the power of
COVENANT

KINGSLEY
FLETCHER

Regal

A Division of Gospel Light
Ventura, California, U.S.A.

Published by Regal Books
A Division of Gospel Light
Ventura, California, U.S.A.
Printed in the U.S.A.

Regal Books is a ministry of Gospel Light, an evangelical Christian publisher dedicated to serving the local church. We believe God's vision for Gospel Light is to provide church leaders with biblical, user-friendly materials that will help them evangelize, disciple and minister to children, youth and families.

It is our prayer that this Regal book will help you discover biblical truth for your own life and help you meet the needs of others. May God richly bless you.

For a free catalog of resources from Regal Books/Gospel Light, please call your Christian supplier or contact us at 1-800-4-GOSPEL *or* www.regalbooks.com.

All Scripture quotations, unless otherwise indicated, are taken from the *Holy Bible, New International Version*®. Copyright © 1973, 1978, 1984 by International Bible Society. Used by permission of Zondervan Publishing House. All rights reserved.

Other version used is:
KJV—King James Version. Authorized King James Version.

Cover Design by Barbara LeVan Fisher
Interior Design by Robert Williams
Edited by Larry Walker

Library of Congress Cataloging-in-Publication Data
Fletcher, Kingsley.
    The power of covenant / Kingsley Fletcher.
        p. cm.
    Includes bibliographical references.
    ISBN 0-8307-2526-1 (trade paper)
      1. Covenant theology.   I. Title.
    BT155 .F53   2000
    231.7'6—dc21   00-055378

1 2 3 4 5 6 7 8 9 10 11 12 13 14 15 / 09 08 07 06 05 04 03 02 01 00

Rights for publishing this book in other languages are contracted by Gospel Literature International (GLINT). GLINT also provides technical help for the adaptation, translation and publishing of Bible study resources and books in scores of languages worldwide. For further information, contact GLINT, P.O. Box 4060, Ontario, CA 91761-1003, U.S.A. You may also send e-mail to Glintint@aol.com, or visit their website at www.glint.org.

contents

section one
THE NATURE OF COVENANT

section two
THE HISTORY OF COVENANT

section three
THE BENEFITS OF COVENANT

section four
CHALLENGES FOR COVENANT THINKING

ACKNOWLEDGMENTS

Covenant relationships have shaped my life from the time I was a small child. What I am today comes from the many people with whom I have had the privilege of being in covenant with—beginning with the greatest keeper of covenant, my Lord Jesus Christ! His undying love for us is the supreme example of genuine relationships.

I also want to acknowledge my parents and siblings—my first covenant brethren. Thank you for all your support and love. You have impacted my life in a grand way.

As my marriage covenant is second only to my covenant with the Lord Jesus Christ, it is most important I recognize my beloved wife, Martha. Thank you for saying "I do" to a lifetime with me! I am also very grateful for the precious relationship I enjoy with my children, Anna, Damaris and Addisu.

Finally, I wish to acknowledge my countless friends in ministry who have stood with me over the years. I wrote this book with you in mind.

the nature of
COVENANT

INTRODUCTION

"Covenant" is a word that very few English-speaking people use today, especially in industrialized nations. In contrast, "covenant" appears hundreds of times in God's Word. It is clear that the New Testament writers assumed their Jewish and predominantly Greek Gentile readers had a deep understanding of covenant principles.

The concept of covenant is prominent in God's Word because *it is the foundation for all of God's promises to mankind.* Covenant principles also serve as the foundation for the government and day-to-day life of God's earthly body, the Church.

I grew up in Ghana, West Africa, where covenant was part of our daily lives. When I moved from my home, I soon learned that very few people understood covenant. Even Christians did not seem to understand the importance of covenant to the success and well-being of the Church. As a result, I have devoted a significant portion of my energies to help the Church recapture and reclaim the power of our covenant in Christ.

As you read this book, fear not! The life of God pulsates through these chapters. You have not picked up a textbook filled with historical and technical data about ancient covenants and treaties of the pre-Christian era. There is a place for such works, but it is not my place to write them.

Press through these pages to discover how you can tap into the power of covenant to bring greater joy and personal fulfillment into your Christian life. God uses covenant relationships to heal our wounds, restore our dreams and transform us into an invincible weapon of light in His hands. Boring? I hope not. Challenging? I am still pressed each time I return to the subject of covenant and the kingdom of God. I pray that this humble tool will help us draw together as a covenant family in His service.

Your covenant brother in Christ,
Dr. Kingsley Fletcher

the nature of
COVENANT

SECTION ONE

rediscover the forgotten
FOUNDATION

CHAPTER 1

In the Eyes of a Prostitute

When I was about 20 years old, I left my homeland of Ghana to preach the gospel in Abidjan, a cosmopolitan city comprised of more than half a million people, in the West African nation of the Ivory Coast. During one of my evangelistic meetings in this former French colony, I met a young lady from Ghana who had come to Abidjan to earn money through prostitution.

She heard me tell the story of God's love and how His Son gave His life on the cross to save us from our sins and restore us to His covenant family. The moment this woman received the message of God's love, an eternal transaction took place. God's love instantly transformed her heart and life, despite the fact that her body was nearly wasted away in the final stages of AIDS by that time.

This prostitute knew she couldn't bring much to God's "bargaining table" because by man's reckoning, she had little to offer or trade in terms of influence, power, abilities or lifetime accomplishments. She came to God knowing she was on the bottom of the social order in that city and in her own homeland. She came to Him as a debtor and He met her as her Redeemer.

This woman knew she couldn't go back to Ghana because prostitution was frowned upon in that culture. She had used much of the proceeds from selling her body in previous years to send her children and her brothers and sisters through high school, and to secure the living of her parents. Her family thought she had a good job in the city, unaware that they would never see her again. Her activities as a prostitute caused her to contract a disease she couldn't even name and now she knew instinctively that death was at her door.

Something else took place in the transaction when she heard the message of Christ and her life was touched. Without much thought or regard for herself, she decided to do something that most religious people would consider repulsive. She just knew she was supposed to give me the remaining money she had earned from prostitution, so I could buy an airline ticket to go abroad and preach the Word of the Lord.

She didn't know me. All she knew was that her life was touched by the Christ that I preached, and in her early existence as a new creature, her thoughts turned away from herself to the lost in other lands. She supernaturally entered into covenant with the One who saved her. He had given all He had for her; now she told me she wanted to invest all that she had in His work.

This Prostitute Taught by Example

This woman of low repute, this street prostitute from the dark byways of Abidjan, taught me by her example just how powerful covenant is and how it operates in our day. I could have refused her gift if I had listened to the religious thoughts in my mind: *After all, that money is tainted. It was earned through prostitution—it isn't worthy of being used in the Lord's work.* Then the Lord spoke to my heart, saying, "It is Me. I am working through this precious woman."

As the woman requested, I used the money she gave me to fly from the Ivory Coast to France where I ministered both to the Portuguese community there and to the prostitutes in that nation's large cities. By God's grace, I was able to share my sponsor's story and final request and led many prostitutes to the Lord. After I lived and ministered in France for a while, the Lord sent me on to England and ultimately the United States.

A born-again prostitute from my homeland was the catalyst. Her covenant gift brought me to where I am today. She is long gone from this earth, but we will meet once again in glory. When I receive the Lord's rewards for the works I've done in this life, I will receive them in her name as well, for she is largely responsible for what I'm doing today.

Shortly after this precious woman gave me her sacrificial gift, she died of AIDS. I knew that by an act of supernatural covenant, I had become her voice to many in other nations. Since that day, I have taken the gospel to many countries of the world and have seen the lives of hundreds of thousands of people changed in cities, towns, villages, churches, auditoriums and marketplaces and in the international business community.

Many of the people who were helped over the years look at me as if I've done something great. If something great has been accomplished, I know it is because of Christ's sacrifice and a redeemed prostitute's covenant gift.

God confirmed this when He led me to Scripture passages concerning another prostitute and her sacrificial gift to Jesus. Even as I write these words, I am reminded afresh that I would not be writing this book today had it not been for the lonely woman who discovered the Way, the Truth and the Life at the end of her physical life in Abidjan.

Covenant Is God's Way

The terminology of covenant may sound foreign or, at the very least, unfamiliar to our ears, yet it is God's way. When I was trying to decide whether or not to accept the gift of a prostitute, the Lord reminded me of the day Jesus was invited to the house of Simon the leper in Bethany. The Scriptures say:

> While Jesus was in Bethany in the home of a man known as Simon the Leper, a woman came to him with an alabaster jar of very expensive perfume, which she poured on his head as he was reclining at the table. When the disciples saw this, they were indignant. "Why this waste?" they asked. "This perfume could have been sold at a high price and the money given to the poor."[1]

Scripture indicates that this woman was a prostitute, yet she was clearly a covenant woman who pleased the Son of God like no other human being before her. We know this because of the way Jesus reacted to her noble action.

Jesus hadn't invited her to this meal in a leper's house. She came on her own despite the highly visible issues in her own life. This woman was considered an outcast because she never went into a man's home without invitation. A prostitute doesn't enter a man's home as a guest. She enters a home for one reason and one reason only: to sell her body for another's illicit pleasure.

An Outcast Came to Do What No One Else Would Do

This prostitute entered Simon's house without invitation. She boldly ignored the disapproving stares and cutting comments of the men seated around her. Evidently she was the only woman in that place, and she came to do something that none of us would ever consider. She emptied an alabaster jar of perfumed anointing oil over the head of Jesus—right in front of everybody.

Every man in the place knew how this woman earned her money, and it took a lot of money to buy that anointing oil. The disciples were so offended and indignant about what this woman did that they openly complained and harshly criticized her for her deed. When they said, "Why this waste?" the original Greek implies they were almost out of control. They were really saying, "Why all this *damnable* waste?"[2] Jesus took an entirely different view:

> Jesus said to them, "Why are you bothering this woman? She has done a beautiful thing to me. The poor you will always have with you, but you will not always have me. When she poured this perfume on my body, she did it to prepare me for burial. I tell you the truth, wherever this gospel is preached throughout the world, what she has done will also be told, in memory of her."[3]

Jesus made it clear that this woman came to prepare His physical body in covenant for His death and resurrection. Jesus wasn't casual or indifferent when He praised this prostitute's humble act of covenant love. He said, "She has done a beautiful thing to me . . . wherever this gospel is preached throughout the world, what she has done will also be told, in memory of her."

I believe this woman saw beyond the natural realm and realized what it means to honor covenant in the spiritual realm. Even though she wasn't there when the covenant was "cut," she looked past her own problems and perceived that Jesus was more than just a great teacher or rabbi. Any other man would have been repulsed by her actions, but something about Jesus was different. She thought, *If I can pour this precious oil on this Man, I can honor His body and the purposes of God He represents.* Little did she know just how timely and important her actions were.

The Covenant Gift of a Prostitute

Jesus praised this woman's kindness before the men that ridiculed her. He made it clear that her gift would be remembered even as the gospel spread throughout the whole world.[4] Her act of selfless sacrifice and bravery prepared the physical body of the Lamb of God for death and for resurrection.

Jesus honored and praised this covenant gift of a prostitute because He knew its true foundation in the spiritual realm and in her heart. She too had come to the Lord's table with little to offer by man's judgment. The worldly worth of her gift was probably considered tainted as well, which may explain the disciples' recommendation that the ointment be sold and the proceeds be distributed to the poor.

The disciples didn't realize that this woman, by faith and by divine direction of the heart, was already reaching beyond her present into the eternity of Christ's covenant. By grace, she was presenting what little she had to honor her Redeemer, who would give His all for her. It was a divine transaction that could not be set aside by the complaints or protests of men. This was the kind of sacrifice that was truly acceptable to God; it was rooted in an eternal, God-initiated blood covenant of redemption.

The act of the born-again prostitute in Abidjan fully illustrated to me how powerful and far-reaching the power of covenant can be, but covenant had always been a part of my life. That was because I grew up in a covenant family and covenant-based culture in Ghana.

Taught to Be My Brother's Keeper

In the Ghanaian culture, large families with close-knit relationships were the norm. I grew up in a home with two parents and eight other children, where relationships were very tight. For as long as I can remember, I was taught that I was my brother's keeper. Even to this day, my family members can hardly wait to get together to talk, laugh and enjoy one another. We grew up with covenant, although we didn't often use the proper name for it. For instance, it is a normal, customary practice in Ghana for family members and close friends to eat together from the same bowl and drink from a common cup.

When I was exposed to the international community, though, I realized that the concept of covenant was not practiced very widely. Many people seemed to protect and isolate themselves from others, and they seemed unwilling to let anyone get close to them. It was as if they were building walls around them to avoid close relationships.

For example, I have seen parents with children and children with parents commuting to some distant location together, yet they still don't know each other. I have watched in amazement as they treated each other like strangers. There was no real relationship there, and it saddened me.

In too many homes, children don't feel they can go to their parents and tell them honestly what is happening in their lives, just as parents don't feel they can tell their children what is happening with them. Covenant-based relationships are different. When we are in covenant, we talk about everything because we understand that the more we know about each other's weakness, the better we are equipped to protect each other. The more we know about each other's strengths, the more we can depend on them when we need help.

> Covenant relationship is the bedrock of God's interaction with mankind.

Many Christians do not realize that the Bible is a book of covenant more than anything else. Covenant relationship is the bedrock of God's interaction with mankind, of Jesus' mission in the flesh to redeem us, and of associations in the Church.

Everything Jesus Did Fulfilled Covenant

It is time for us to rediscover the forgotten foundations of our faith in Christ. Everything Jesus did in His earthly ministry was God's fulfillment of covenant promises He made to mankind long ago. We serve a covenant-keeping God. The way Jesus dealt with His disciples was a continuous picture of covenant relationship in action. If this is so, why have we seemingly lost all understanding of the power of covenant in most of our modern churches and in our individual lives?

The absence of covenant in the Church really became an issue to me when I realized that many people in church circles who said "I like you" or "I love you, Kingsley," actually said it because of what they perceived my position to be—a leader among my people in Ghana.

Today, I realize that many people are quick to say "I love you," when they are merely impressed or attracted to a person's credentials, social status or spiritual notoriety. Perhaps they hear a name mentioned in association with the names of other nationally known ministers, and they think, *If I could be around this person, perhaps he could help me to get to the next level.*

Do not look for genuine relationship in flattering words.[5] In the absence of true covenant relationship, people tend to like you *only as long as you maintain their expectations.* However, the moment they find out that you are not what they expected or wanted you to be, they abandon you.

The problem has to do with covenant—the forgotten foundation of lasting friendships, true kinship in God's kingdom and unity of effort in public service and business enterprises. Where there is no covenant, people tend to put self above another needs or cares.

Covenant Isn't a Cultural Concept—It Is a Heavenly Pattern
I was surprised to learn that most people in Western industrialized nations basically don't understand covenant. It seems like it is a foreign concept in these cultures. On the contrary, I believe the Bible teaches that covenant isn't a cultural concept—it is a heavenly pattern for enduring and fruitful earthly relationships. It transcends the ever-changing whims and notions of mankind. In fact, I am convinced that covenant is God's pri-

mary means of bringing stability and security into the brief and often chaotic lives of men and women.

My burden and challenge is to help as many as I can in the Body of Christ to understand and rediscover the power of covenant. I often start by recalling the examples set by a select few in the West who really did understand covenant and devoted their lives to living it out. Many years ago as a young man from the African nation of Ghana, my life was transformed by the gospel of Jesus Christ. The good news found its way into my distant continent because of the covenant of Christian missionaries from America and other countries in the Western hemisphere. I know that even before I met the prostitute in Abidjan, these spiritual fathers were also responsible for who I am and where I serve today. Now my life's work in Christ is to return their covenant sacrifice by delivering the hope of the gospel to their children's children in their own land.

My entire family benefited from the covenant these light-skinned fathers made unto God. They demonstrated that covenant by dying on my shores and giving me and my people hope to live again in Christ. I was reborn because these godly covenant keepers gave me a blessed hope in Jesus Christ. Now the principles of covenant call me to remember their sacrifice of love and to live up to the heritage they gave me in Christ's name.

Like the prostitutes in Bethany and Abidjan, we come to God having little to offer in the bargain. It seems like the full weight of the covenants of God rest upon His broad shoulders. Those who are familiar with covenant will tell you that is the way it should be. In most cases, the one who offers covenant is the greater, while those who receive the benefits of covenant are the lesser of the parties. This is *always* true in the covenants between God and man.

When we rediscover the forgotten foundations of covenant, our homes will be blessed, our marriages will be stronger, our children will be better adjusted and secure in the world, our churches will thrive in an atmosphere of unity in Christ, and our businesses will prosper as never before. The reason is that true covenant causes our personal relationships to bloom under the light of true love and commitment—I am talking about the God-kind-of-love that is unconditional while being fully aware of our shortcomings.

The power of covenant will revolutionize every aspect of human life (exactly as God intended it should), *if* we allow it to do so. Covenant relationships require commitment and consistency, but as we will see in the chapters ahead, the benefits offered to us by the covenants and covenant principles of God are beyond calculation.

Notes
1. Matthew 26:6-9.
2. James Strong, *Strong's Exhaustive Concordance of the Bible* (Peabody, MA: Hendrickson Publishers, n.d.), meanings and definitions drawn from the word derivations for the noun "waste" (Greek, #684, 622).
3. Matthew 26:10-13.
4. See Matthew 26:13.
5. See Proverbs 29:5; Romans 16:18; 1 Thessalonians 2:5.

God's early
COVENANTS
with humanity

CHAPTER 2

Covenants and Promises

The Bible is filled with God's promises concerning our welfare, health, finances, children, destinies and much, much more. Most of the teaching in our churches centers around selected individual promises God has made to us, and this is not necessarily bad. I think it is better, however, to approach the promises of God through the controlling contracts that govern them all. I am talking about the covenants of God.

There is a difference between a promise of God and a covenant of God. The covenants of God reveal the nature of God's relationship with us and the climate of conditions in which the covenants were cut. A covenant is typically built upon several promises grouped together for a very specific purpose, and it is the covenant which reveals that purpose.

A promise can be made by anyone to anyone else without making a genuine commitment to relationship. Promises can be casually made to a stranger, to a business acquaintance or to a foreign government. By definition, a promise is "a declaration that one will do or refrain from doing something specified, or a legally binding declaration that gives the person to whom it is made a right to expect or to claim the performance or forbearance of a specified act."[1]

Generally, promises are only as good as the character of the person making the promise (or the level of fear created by the legally binding consequences of breaking that promise). Promises of all kinds are freely broken every day by individuals, groups, businesspeople, corporations and even governments.

A covenant, on the other hand, can only be made between two or more parties in relationship to one another. A covenant is too serious to be entered into lightly, so covenants are not made with just anyone. Although some promises are similar to covenants, they are not the same, even though every covenant contains promises.

Covenant Still Carries Deeper Meanings Today

The modern Western definition for covenant is "a usually formal, solemn, and binding agreement: a compact; a written agreement or promise usually under seal between two or more parties especially for the performance of some action."[2] Among the ancient covenant peoples of the Middle East, the Far East and Africa, covenant still carries deeper meanings and responsibilities that are not easily translated into legalese or court documents.

Let me begin with the greatest of all of God's covenants with mankind and then move backward in time to the beginning of God's involvement with the human race. Consider these insights from the book of Hebrews:

But the ministry Jesus has received is as superior to theirs as the covenant of which he is mediator is superior to the old one, and it is founded on better promises. For if there had been nothing wrong with that first covenant, no place would have been sought for another. But God found fault with the people and said: "The time is coming, declares the Lord, when I will make a new covenant with the house of Israel and with the house of Judah. It will not be like the covenant I made with their forefathers when I took them by the hand to lead them out of Egypt, because they did not remain faithful to my covenant, and I turned away from them, declares the Lord. This is the covenant I will make with the house of Israel after that time, declares the Lord. I will put my laws in their minds and write them on their hearts. I will be their God, and they will be my people. No longer will a man teach his neighbor, or a man his brother, saying, 'Know the Lord.'"[3]

Genesis Contains the Roots of Covenant

As with virtually everything else in creation, this covenant and all others can be traced back to the book of Genesis and God's first interaction with Adam and Eve whom He created. God the

Father revealed the roots of covenant even as He discoursed with God the Son, and later in His statements to the couple:

> Then God said, "Let us make man in our image, in our likeness, and let them rule over the fish of the sea and the birds of the air, over the livestock, over all the earth, and over all the creatures that move along the ground." So God created man in his own image, in the image of God he created him; male and female he created them. God blessed them and said to them, "Be fruitful and increase in number; fill the earth and subdue it. Rule over the fish of the sea and the birds of the air and over every living creature that moves on the ground." Then God said, "I give you every seed-bearing plant on the face of the whole earth and every tree that has fruit with seed in it. They will be yours for food. And to all the beasts of the earth and all the birds of the air and all the creatures that move on the ground—everything that has the breath of life in it—I give every green plant for food." And it was so.[4]

This passage of Scripture contains the first covenant God made with man. It differs from the covenants that follow it in one important respect: there are no curses or consequences attached to it. Adam and Eve had not yet fallen into sin, so this covenant contains God's promises, instructions and blessings without any mention of curses or consequences associated with breaking the covenant.

Adam's Covenant

The covenants of God build upon one another toward a predetermined end. The second covenant appears when God placed

Adam in the garden He had made. Again, this covenant lacks the formality and structure apparent in later post-Edenic covenants, but this particular covenant was the first in the history of mankind to contain a warning. With these words, God established the first boundary for the man He created:

> The LORD God took the man and put him in the Garden of Eden to work it and take care of it. And the LORD God commanded the man, "You are free to eat from any tree in the garden; but *you must not* eat from the tree of the knowledge of good and evil, for *when you eat of it you will surely die.*"[5]

Through this covenant, God moved Adam in specific position in the Garden of Eden, gave him even more detailed instructions about his assignment, outlined key privileges and freedoms he enjoyed, and then gave him a solemn warning about the tree of the knowledge of good and evil. We know this was a covenant because of what happened when the warning was ignored and the covenant broken. The repercussions sound amazingly like the cursings or consequences portion of later covenants:

> So the LORD God said to the serpent, "Because you have done this, cursed are you above all the livestock and all the wild animals! You will crawl on your belly and you will eat dust all the days of your life. And I will put enmity between you and the woman, and between your offspring and hers; he will crush your head, and you will strike his heel." To the woman he said, "I will greatly increase your pains in childbearing; with pain you will give birth to children. Your desire will be for your

husband, and he will rule over you." To Adam he said, "Because you listened to your wife and ate from the tree about which I commanded you, 'You must not eat of it,' cursed is the ground because of you; through painful toil you will eat of it all the days of your life. It will produce thorns and thistles for you, and you will eat the plants of the field. By the sweat of your brow you will eat your food until you return to the ground."[6]

Notice that God had not changed Adam's assignment; He simply moved him out of His personal garden and into the world outside of Eden. He also removed His covering of divine favor and cursed the ground upon which Adam depended for food and provisions. It seemed that nature itself would now work against Adam and his descendants.

Adam's pre-Fall assignment from God in Genesis 1:28 was a portion of his divine destiny that remained with him even after he and Eve were expelled from the Garden of Eden. They were still created and called to multiply, rule and exercise dominion in the earth.

As the acceptance of Abel's sacrifice demonstrated a few years later, God was just as willing to bless and be blessed by His creation as He was in the garden, but obedience and a pure heart were required, mixed with the shed blood of an innocent sacrifice as an atonement for man's sin. The shedding of blood would mark all major covenants between God and man and among men. Finally it took the very blood of the Lamb of God, who would come to offer Himself once and for all, to establish the greatest covenant of all.

God made a minor covenant with Cain after God banished him from civilization for murdering his brother, Abel. He promised that no man who found Cain alone in the years to come would murder him because God would place a mark or a sign upon him.[7] This was the first sign to physically confirm and mark a covenant of God.

Noah's Covenant

For some time God enjoyed intimate relationships with men after Abel's murder. The Bible tells us that after Adam and Eve's third son, Seth, saw his first son born, that "men began to call on the name of the LORD."[8] We know that Enoch, a descendant of Seth, walked with God in intimate fellowship for 300 years or more. The Bible says, "Enoch walked with God; then he was no more, because God took him away."[9] Noah, Enoch's great-grandson, carried on in his great-grandfather's tradition, for the Bible says, "Noah was a righteous man, blameless among the people of his time, *and he walked with God.*"[10]

When the waters of the great flood receded and Noah offered a burnt sacrifice to God, the Lord established His first formal covenant with mankind. That covenant contains many of the foundational promises by which we live today:

> The LORD smelled the pleasing aroma and said in his heart: "Never again will I curse the ground because of man, even though every inclination of his heart is evil from childhood. And never again will I destroy all living creatures, as I have done. As long as the earth endures, seedtime and harvest, cold and heat, summer and winter, day and night will never cease."[11]

The first phrases in God's answer to Noah's sweet-smelling sacrifice reveal two aspects of progressive covenants: God used later covenants to remove specific elements from earlier covenants (in this case, He removed the original curse on the land found in Genesis 3:17), and He also used them to clarify or add to His promises in earlier covenants.

In this passage, He declares what we refer to as the law of seedtime and harvest—a law that encompasses both the physical and spiritual realms to this day. God went on to reinforce to Noah the basic tenets of the original dominion and rule commission He gave to Adam, and He mentioned specific details in this covenant with Noah:

> Then God said to Noah and to his sons with him: *"I now establish my covenant with you and with your descendants after you and with every living creature that was with you*—the birds, the livestock and all the wild animals, all those that came out of the ark with you . . . Never again will all life be cut off by the waters of a flood; never again will there be a flood to destroy the earth." And God said, "This is the sign of the covenant I am making between me and you and every living creature with you, a covenant for all generations to come: I have set my rainbow in the clouds, and it will be the sign of the covenant between me and the earth."[12]

The Covenantal Rainbow of God's Grace

You and I still benefit from this covenant God established with Noah at the second beginning of the human race. The rainbow sign, and the covenant promise it illustrates, reveals some of the early covenantal foundations for the grace God extends toward people of all races, colors and ethnic origins.

After the Flood, the human race expanded and gradually divided into three groups descended from Noah's three sons and their wives. Sadly, the knowledge of God seemed to be diminishing as the human population grew. The only covenants in operation appeared to be man-made covenants that were solely built upon mutual benefit and acquisition of power, fame or money. I say this because the massive public building project known as the Tower of Babel could only be proposed by a large number of people who were united with one purpose and goal in mind (for better or for worse) which speaks of an operational covenant in effect. That spoken covenant of agreement appears in Genesis 11:4. Nothing else could bring together so many people and such human effort and building resources in unity. God moved to destroy the power of human unity by dispersing the people into different language groups.

After that, God seemed to have little contact with mankind until He appeared to Abram, a descendant of Noah's son, Shem. God asked Abram to leave his father's household and follow Him; then He made a simple verbal covenant containing what we recognize today as a Messianic prophecy: "and *all peoples on earth will be blessed through you*" (see quote below). Abram was 75 years old when he heard God say:

> The LORD had said to Abram, "Leave your country, your people and your father's household and go to the land I will show you. I will *make you into a great nation* and I will *bless you*; I will *make your name great*, and *you will be a blessing*. I will *bless those who bless you*, and *whoever curses you I will curse*; and *all peoples on earth will be blessed through you*."[13]

God's Seven-Part Covenant to Abram

This simple seven-part covenant forms the foundation for much of what follows in the Word of God and in the world of men. As often happens with the covenants and communications of God, when Abraham obeyed God's command to leave his people and his father's house behind (specifically speaking of his grown nephew, Lot, at this point), God expounded upon and expanded His original covenantal promises to Abram. Only *obedience* can take us forward from God's original covenant promises to the next level in His plan:

> The LORD said to Abram *after Lot had parted from him*, "Lift up your eyes from where you are and look north and south, east and west. All the land that you see I will give to you and your offspring forever. I will make your offspring like the dust of the earth, so that if anyone could count the dust, then your offspring could be counted. Go, walk through the length and breadth of the land, for I am giving it to you." So Abram moved his tents and went to live near the great trees of Mamre at Hebron, where he built an altar to the LORD.[14]

Over many years, God's covenant with Abram would satisfy a need for reassurance in the fulfillment of those promises He made. That desire for the promises to be made real fashioned in Abram reliance, trust and faith in his relationship with God. While everyone else worshiped man-made gods of wood, stone and other materials (which could easily be seen and touched), Abram based his actions and future upon a covenant of promises made by an unseen God.

God's Expanded Covenant

Although considerable time had passed, Abram still had no heir, and he needed reassurance. God once again expanded and expounded upon the details or the how-tos of His covenant with Abram. The last verse of this passage is one of the most familiar Old Testament passages in the Bible and is quoted in the apostle Paul's letter to the Galatians as well:

> But Abram said, "O Sovereign LORD, what can you give me since I remain childless and the one who will inherit my estate is Eliezer of Damascus?" And Abram said, "You have given me no children; so a servant in my household will be my heir." Then the word of the LORD came to him: "This man will not be your heir, but a son coming from your own body will be your heir." He took him outside and said, "Look up at the heavens and count the stars—if indeed you can count them." Then he said to him, "So shall your offspring be." *Abram believed the LORD, and he credited it to him as righteousness.*[15]

Abram's life is marked by a pattern: God speaks in covenant blessing, Abram obeys the ordinances of the covenant; God blesses in further covenant blessing, Abram offers a sacrifice of thanksgiving or obeys yet another ordinance; and God expands the blessings of the covenant even further. Perhaps we can learn something from Abram's approach to the covenants of God.

After God credited Abram's faith as righteousness, He set out to bless Abram even more. He began the process by declaring His purpose for bringing Abram out of his father's land: He was going to give him possession of the land He had promised. Abram was still beset with the human weakness of unbelief, and he asked God, "O Sovereign LORD, how can I know that I will gain possession of it?"[16]

God's answer was to establish the most famous and far-reaching covenant in human history—until the day Jesus Christ established a newer and greater covenant in His own blood. Yet even then, when the Lord established the new covenant in Christ's blood, He did not do away with the Abrahamic covenant; He extended the blessings of this covenant of faith beyond the bounds of Judaism to the Gentiles, as the apostle Paul later made clear.

> The Scripture foresaw that God would justify the Gentiles by faith, and announced the gospel in advance to Abraham: "All nations will be blessed through you." So those who have faith are blessed along with Abraham, the man of faith.
>
> All who rely on observing the law are under a curse, for it is written: "Cursed is everyone who does not continue to do everything written in the Book of the Law." Clearly no one is justified before God by the law, because, "The righteous will live by faith." The law is not based on faith; on the contrary, "The man who does these things will live by them." Christ redeemed us from the curse of the law by becoming a curse for us, for it is written: "Cursed is everyone who is hung on a tree." He redeemed us in order that the blessing given to Abraham might come to the Gentiles through Christ Jesus, so that by faith we might receive the promise of the Spirit.[17]

The Lord cut a formal covenant with Abram by passing through the cloven bodies of a heifer, a goat, a ram, a dove and a young pigeon in strict accordance with the covenantal ordinances of that day.[18] The covenant was fixed in Abram's mind and he knew it was an eternally binding agreement for both parties.

Conforming Abram's Name to His Covenant Identity

Nearly 14 years later (or 13 years after Ishmael was born to Abram through the servant girl, Hagar), God again visited Abram to formally change his name to Abraham. He set apart Abraham's entire household and future heirs as holy, and delivered to Abraham the Old Testament ordinance of the physical circumcision of all males.[19]

Once we begin to honor the covenants God makes with us individually and as His Church corporately, we can expect to undergo major changes in how we are known by God and by other people. We can expect unnecessary things and hurtful things to be cut away from our lives as we are set apart for holy purposes in line with our covenant life in Christ.

There are many other covenants in the Bible, some of which we will examine in later chapters. There is one final covenant we need to examine before we move on, however, because this covenant reveals what happens when a man with no reputation, power, money or credentials grows unquenchably hungry for the abiding presence of God. I am talking about David, of course. This man began his covenant journey as a lowly shepherd boy singing praises to God alone in the sheep fields. His love and devotion so moved God that He moved heaven and earth to elevate this shepherd from a sheep field to the palace of a king. God even ordained that His only begotten Son would take on the earthly name, "Son

When we honor God's covenants with us, we can expect major changes in our relationships.

of David," in honor of this beloved worshiper and faithful covenant partner!

Many of the greatest promises contained under the new covenant of Christ's blood can be traced to God's original covenant with David. As the apostle Paul told Jewish listeners in a synagogue in Antioch:

> After removing Saul, he [God] made David their king. He testified concerning him: "I have found David son of Jesse *a man after my own heart; he will do everything I want him to do.*" From this man's descendants God has brought to Israel the Savior Jesus, *as he promised.*[20]

David's Covenant

David's love and single-minded devotion to God made him a true worshiper in an apostate era. He personally restored the ark of God and the divine presence it represented to its central place in the life and focus of Israel, and demanded that Israel return to the God of their fathers. Because he honored the covenants of God cut with Abraham, Isaac and Jacob (Israel), God, in turn, made a special covenant with David:

> When your days are over and you go to be with your fathers, I will raise up your offspring to succeed you, one of your own sons, and I will establish his kingdom. He is the one who will build a house for me, and I will establish his throne forever. I will be his father, and he will be my son. I will never take my love away from him, as I took it away from your predecessor. I will set him over my house and my kingdom forever; his throne will be established forever.[21]

God knew from the beginning that He would send His Son to fulfill the greatest of all covenants at Golgotha in Jerusalem in the fullness of time. His original intention was for Adam and all of his seed to walk in fellowship with Him and to enjoy His continual blessings. Due to the consequences of man's sin, God ultimately chose to work through a remnant of Abraham's seed (the Jewish people) to bring His Son into the earth.

Finally, He narrowed down the field to the bloodline of the greatest worshiper in the history of mankind. It was from the house of David that God would bring forth His Deliverer. In the end, Jesus Christ entered our world as God's covenant solution to bring representatives of all the nations together again under His blood.

Every great promise, purpose and act of God can be traced, linked or proven to be clearly foreshadowed or ordained in the covenants God made with mankind. Each successive covenant builds upon those that went before, yet all of the covenants can be traced to the first great covenants God made in the book of Genesis.

Notes
 1. *Merriam-Webster's Collegiate Dictionary*, 10th ed., s.v. "promise."
 2. Ibid, p. 267.
 3. Hebrews 8:6-11.
 4. Genesis 1:26-30.
 5. Genesis 2:15-17, italics mine.
 6. Genesis 3:14-19.
 7. See Genesis 4:8-15.
 8. Genesis 4:26.
 9. Genesis 5:24.
 10. Genesis 6:9, italics mine.
 11. Genesis 8:21,22.
 12. Genesis 9:8-13, italics mine.
 13. Genesis 12:1-3, italics mine.

14. Genesis 13:14-17, italics mine.
15. Genesis 15:2-6, italics mine; see also Galatians 3:6.
16. Genesis 15:8.
17. Galatians 3:8-14.
18. See Genesis 15:9-21.
19. See Genesis 17.
20. Acts 13:22,23, italics mine.
21. 1 Chronicles 17:11-14, parallel to 2 Samuel 7:12,13. This passage is also cited in Psalm 132.

what makes a
COVENANT?

CHAPTER 3

Security and Faithfulness

Many of the books, seminary courses and Bible studies available on the subject of covenant focus on the technical aspects of the covenant process. Some of these books are written by born-again Christians who genuinely love God and reverence His Word. Others are written by professional scholars who may or may not believe in God and who just happen to concentrate on religious, anthropological, archaeological or sociological patterns in the Bible.

The latter group tends to approach the study of covenant with all of the faith and spiritual interest of fossils. In their books, covenant is usually analyzed, compartmentalized and dissected like the lifeless remains of something found only in the ancient past.

The power of covenant living has also been largely lost in the modern Church. The academicians are correct to assume that, in most cases, the modern Christian experience often includes only lifeless remains of what once was covenant.

However, covenant is alive and well in the heart, purposes and plans of God for this generation. For that reason, we must look at covenant through the lens of faith and the clarifying optics of the Holy Spirit. There is another reason to study covenant as well: It benefits us and transforms our lives.

Covenant living perfectly positions us for blessings and provision by preserving godly attitudes and encouraging godly actions toward the Lord and toward other people. The comparison between covenant living and life without covenant principles is almost identical to the comparison between those who supposedly "get saved" (as if it were a one-time event requiring no further action, obedience to God's Word or interaction with the Savior) and those who become lifetime disciples of Jesus Christ. In fact, the covenant life is simply the life of a true disciple of Jesus Christ.

That which is spirit cannot be discerned by that which is of the flesh, and people who don't begin their study of covenant from the foundation that God created all things, will be at a loss to understand true covenant.

The Influence of Faith in Understanding Covenant

Professional scholars who study the Bible strictly are fond of comparing the covenants in the Bible to classical Near Eastern treaties used by Hittite kings to bring vassal nations under their control. Some of them imply that Hebrew scribes simply copied the key components of the Hittite treaties of their day and concocted high-sounding covenants in God's name to impress the people under their sway.

The ancient Hittite treaties dating from 1500 to 600 B.C. do have some similar components to Old Testament covenants. It is possible that the Hittites and other early civilizations copied the basic elements of covenant structure from the covenants God made with various leaders in that era, such as Noah, Abraham, Isaac, Jacob/Israel and others. The main point is that God is the author of covenants regardless of whether it was invented by the Hittites or the Jews.

There are at least four basic components to a formal biblical covenant: a *history* describing how the parties to the covenant are linked to one another, a list of the *responsibilities* of the partners to the covenant, a *covenant renewal clause* describing the document or covenant and requiring that it be read or rehearsed publicly at regular times, and the *blessings and curses* received by those who keep or break the covenant, respectively.

All four of these formal covenant components are found in the Mosaic covenant as outlined in the book of Deuteronomy. Chapters 1–3 describe the history of God's relationship with Moses and the Israelites, and chapters 4–46 describe the responsibilities of each of the parties to the covenant. Chapter 27 serves as the "the covenant renewal clause," prescribing how often the covenant is to be read; and chapter 28 is the well-known description of the blessings and curses attached to the Mosaic covenant.

Count the Ways I Will Bless You

Blessings and curses are two forces at work behind the scenes in every covenant. They govern the earthly execution of our covenant agreements with God in heaven. The foundation of blessing was laid when God made a covenant with Abraham concerning his seed.[1]

Four hundred and thirty years later, God sent Moses to keep His promise and deliver Abraham's seed or descendants from Egyptian bondage, and He renewed the Abrahamic covenant with an expanded Mosaic covenant.[2] That covenant included the giving of the Law and a call for the descendants of Abraham to become a nation unto God for the first time in history.

After 40 years of wandering in the wilderness, a disobedient generation died out and Moses declared or rehearsed anew to the Israelites the blessings listed in Deuteronomy 28, just before the Israelites crossed the river Jordan into the Promised Land. These covenant promises should be of special interest to Christians because believers have inherited these same Deuteronomic promises—which are extensions of God's covenant to Abraham—by faith through Christ:

> If you fully obey the LORD your God and carefully follow all his commands I give you today, the LORD your God will set you high above all the nations on earth. All these blessings will come upon you and accompany you if you obey the LORD your God: *You will be blessed in the city and blessed in the country. The fruit of your womb will be blessed, and the crops of your land and the young of your livestock—the calves of your herds and the lambs of your flocks. Your basket and your kneading trough will be blessed. You will be blessed when you come in and blessed when you go out.* The LORD will grant that the enemies who rise up against you will be defeated before you. They will come at you from one direction but flee from you in seven. The LORD will send a blessing on your barns and on everything you put your hand to. The LORD your God will bless you in the land he is giving you.

The LORD will establish you as his holy people, as he promised you on oath, if you keep the commands of the LORD your God and walk in his ways. Then all the peoples on earth will see that you are called by the name of the LORD, and they will fear you. The LORD will open the heavens, the storehouse of his bounty, to send rain on your land in season and to bless all the work of your hands. You will lend to many nations but will borrow from none. The LORD will make you the head, not the tail. If you pay attention to the commands of the LORD your God that I give you this day and carefully follow them, you will always be at the top, never at the bottom.[3]

For many years, Christians mistakenly believed these blessings passed away with the new covenant in Christ; but as we noted earlier, Paul makes it clear that Jesus extended this covenant of Abraham's blessing to all "children of faith."[4]

The unseen components in a true biblical covenant are far more important than the formal outward aspects of written covenant documents. For instance, Jesus summed up the spirit of covenant in the unforgettable phrase: "Greater love has no one than this, that he lay down his life for his friends."[5]

The reality of covenant, or the real outward proof of covenant life in action, is the presence of genuine truth and honesty in the relationships between the covenant partners. If you and I are in covenant, then our communications with one another should demonstrate a consistent level of truth and honesty, no matter what circumstances we face at any particular time.

The First Covenants

The first covenants God made were with individuals who enjoyed an intimate relationship with Him (later covenants were made with the people as a whole). These initial covenants tended to be brief, simple and heavily weighted toward the blessings. Some of them don't even contain a "cursings" clause. This is an indication of the kind of relationship these individuals had with God.

As the covenants were renewed with their growing families or succeeding generations, or with the group of people associated with the original covenant holders, the relationships these second generation groups had with the Lord tended to be shallower and typified by the question, What's in it for me? (Does this sound familiar?) At the same time, the length, complexity and "curses" sections of the covenants grew longer as the legal aspect took precedent over personal relationship.

One of the reasons I've written this book is to help the Church in general, and you and I specifically, reclaim the intimate and personal relationship with God that fuels the power of true covenant life. Covenant has passed out of the daily lives of Christians because intimacy and personal relationship with God Himself have faded away from generation to generation. It is time for us to reverse this downward spiral toward alienation from one another and from intimacy with God. It all begins with a choice, and there are many reasons why we should choose the covenant life in Christ.

Covenant relationships in Christ supply the building blocks of joy in human relationships. This is the way God designed it to be. Covenant living provides that vital sense of *security and faithfulness* that most people lack in their lives. We expend vast amounts of energy, money and resources trying to find the covenant life we were created to enjoy. It doesn't have to be this way.

Because the Church has largely abandoned covenant living, people have sought the benefits of covenant life wherever and however they can find them. The benefits of covenant include security, assurance, protection and hope. I suspect that a hunger for covenant relationship—and a void of these relationships in the Church—has led many adults in the United States to turn to secret Masonic societies or to nonsectarian civic service organizations in a search for covenant closeness and belonging.

New Testament Covenant Patterns Are Neglected

The sad truth is that the modern culture is far removed from the social end of the New Testament patterns: community lifestyles rooted in intimate covenant relationships and marked by caring, sharing, giving and receiving in mutual commitment to one another. This has created a void that has many destructive consequences. It is a fundamental principle in both the natural and spiritual realms that where there is a void, something will be found to fill it (for better or for worse).

For example, universally, youth are especially hungry for close, covenant relationships with their peers and with caring adults. There is no better place for these covenant relationships than in the home and in the local church. When young people don't have these kinds of relationships in these traditional safe havens, they search for relationships elsewhere. As a result, this nation has seen an incredible rise in the number, size and activities of street gangs over the last 20 years.

Young people hunger for covenantal security and bonding, and increasingly they seem to be turning to gang life to fill the void for covenant fellowship and a genuine sense of family. Don't expect them to give you a long, detailed description of what they are looking for. All they know is that they want to show or demonstrate their loyalty to one another. They are after an outward expression of covenant, and you can see it in any public or private school in America.

Whether the subjects are teenage girls, boys, preteens or college students, they can be observed congregating in groups as if directed by an invisible hand. Whatever draws them together, they are all covenant seekers. They are seeking people who can and will be part of their covenant or "brothers of a common bond."

Numerous television documentaries on American teens have featured young persons saying something such as, "I was part of this group, but then they decided they didn't like me." More often than not, the interviewers have asked the young people how they felt about the rejection, and many have admitted that they felt like killing themselves when they discovered they no longer belonged to their group (their covenant family).

Everyone Wants to Belong

Everyone wants to feel like they are a part of a covenant family. It doesn't matter how old we are, how mature we believe ourselves to be or how successful we may be in our chosen profession or occupation. We still want to belong.

The search for covenant belonging is pervasive. If you go to lunch in any medium-to-large city in America, you will see throngs of businesspeople sitting across tables, having lunch and sharing some of the most intimate things in their lives. It is a fact that the person with whom you spend the most time sharing meals and talking across a table is the person most likely to know everything you are feeling. Unfortunately, family members and fellow church members rarely make this intimate sharing list.

We instinctively share our feelings during a meal (even men do it) with peers. We need to see the same kind of sharing take place at the family dinner table during the evening meal. That may require us to shift schedules or turn off the television to eat together around a common table. It is there that we can find out what is going on in one another's hearts.

It is a fact that the people with whom we share covenant often know more about us at times than our parents do. That isn't wrong; it is natural. True covenant—as differentiated from what I call "covenants of convenience"—provides a level of trust and love that encourages honesty in astonishing ways. It is a fact that true covenant keepers are secret protectors.

Where Are the Covenant Keepers?

Contrast this picture with the cutthroat profit mentality that rules businesses, dominates the entertainment industry and fuels our shallow self-centered relationships. Such a mentality infiltrates every aspect of society. It isn't pleasant to admit this, but it even enters the Church! Where are the covenant keepers?

This is frightening when we consider consequences to this admission. The apostle Paul described the last days this way:

> There will be terrible times in the last days. People will be lovers of themselves, lovers of money, boastful, proud, abusive, disobedient to their parents, ungrateful, unholy, without love, unforgiving [the authorized *King James Version* more accurately translates this as "*trucebreakers*"[6]], slanderous, without self-control, brutal, not lovers of the good, treacherous, rash, conceited, lovers of pleasure rather than lovers of God—having a form of godliness but denying its power. Have nothing to do with them.[7]

Any nation that reaches the state where lawyers and stacks of legal documents are needed for even the simplest of sales or purchase agreements is a nation that has lost its covenant roots. Where truth and honesty are replaced by widespread falsehood and dishonesty, the penalties and "curses" section of every contract will far outweigh the sections listing the benefits of an agreement.

We have forgotten that when we betray a covenant, we curse ourselves. Suppose someone goes to a friend and confesses a personal weakness. Then the trusted friend promises to protect his friend while helping him correct the problem. If the trusted friend chooses to use that privileged information against the man later on, the Bible says that even while he is digging a pit for his friend, the betrayer will fall into the pit himself.[8] It is a serious thing to break covenant, whether we realize it or not.

Someone recently told me that the United States Navy teaches covenant principles to candidates and operational members of the Navy SEALs, its elite special forces component.[9] Even the basic training regimen for the SEALs is dangerous, but the kinds of all-weather, nighttime military operations these men are trained to conduct are extremely hazardous. One of the most rigid rules drilled into every SEAL is *Never leave your buddy*. The SEALs always work in pairs, and in groups of pairs within tightly knit field units. A Navy SEAL will lay down his life to save his partner if necessary, but above all he will never leave him behind or abandon him. This is a good picture of covenant relationship in action.

What Is the Value of Loyalty?

Whether we examine the lives of people who belong to a tight-knit social group or members of a street gang, they all seem to have a deep understanding of the value of *loyalty* to their friends and covenant partners. This issue is so important to them that many gang members literally would rather die than betray their friends. In other words, they would die to protect their covenant relationships. Does that sound familiar? Remember the words of Jesus we noted earlier: "Greater love has no one than this, that he lay down his life for his friends."[10]

It is said that on the western frontiers of America a century ago, a man's word was his bond. It was considered a fighting affair to challenge the worth of a man's word in the Old West, because a man's reputation was all that he had. Large land sales, livestock transactions and business deals were all conducted on the basis of a man's personal word and a handshake. To conduct business on that basis today is unthinkable, but wouldn't it be nice if God's people once again reached that level of personal integrity and honesty?

In the coming years, unless the trend changes, we are going to bring a curse upon this millennium through our truce-breaking ways. God has called the Church out of the world to be a shining light set on a hill. We are called to live as a community bound together by covenant love. That kind of living will set us apart in this day and age!

The only way we can reclaim our heritage as the family of God in the earth is to restore the foundations of covenant lifestyle to our lives. It means we will have to obey the commands of Jesus instead of giving them lip service only. When Jesus prayed that we would love one another, we should take the hint that He was praying God's perfect will for born-again believers.

The potential for growth and risk taking is unlimited when we are supported by loyal friends who love us enough to give us the right to fail—without fear of being rejected or cast aside. This kind of unconditional love is all too rare in the ranks of the Church today. Why? We don't understand or value covenant.

Covenant Is Love with No Strings Attached

True covenant relationships provide the vital building blocks of security and faithfulness to our homes and our local churches. We feel more secure because there are no "strings attached" to the love we receive from our covenant family. We are loved in spite of our shortcomings and faults, exactly as Jesus loves us. We feel safe because we belong to something larger and more powerful than ourselves. This is especially true in view of the fact that God Himself is the foundation and leading covenant partner in our "family."

> Covenant relationships include a built-in level of personal accountability.

Covenant creates faithfulness in us individually because it births a deep desire to bring honor and joy to our covenant family and its individual members. When we take to heart the principles of our covenant in Christ, we would rather die than fail or betray our Master and our brethren in the faith. Missionaries and martyrs demonstrate this kind of loyalty and faithfulness to Christ every week across the globe.

Covenant relationships include a built-in level of personal accountability because we relate to one another with a disarming honesty that strips away facades and falsehood. In a true covenant environment, we feel free to admit our failures and recurring challenges in life because we know we won't be rejected for our honesty. Then our covenant partners feel free to speak the truth in love to help us overcome our failures while walking with us through the difficulties. This is covenant living in Christ at its best.

Covenant Is a "God Thing"

The concept of covenant runs throughout the Bible. It isn't respective to a particular group of people. It is a "God thing" that permeates everything He does with us. In fact, the concept of covenant even permeates the secular world and shows up in every society of man in one form or another. Some societies have done a better job than others of burying their covenantal roots.

The truth is that the gospel is about covenant—it is the good news of God's new covenant with man sealed in Christ's precious blood. In fact, the Bible says:

> For this reason *Christ is the mediator of a new covenant*, that those who are called may receive the promised eternal inheritance—now that he has died as a ransom to set them free from the sins committed under the first covenant.[11]

The power of God's greatest covenant with mankind is found in the blood of His Son, Jesus Christ. He rose from the dead and now serves as mediator of that same covenant of grace. The Church must rediscover her awe and reverence for the cost of her freedom.

Some of the covenants of God are unconditional. God makes a promise, and He fulfills that promise regardless of the cooperation of His people. God told David his heir would have an everlasting kingdom; God promised to Jeremiah that He would establish a new covenant with His people.[12] Neither of these covenants were dependent in any way on the faithfulness or obedience of God's people. In fact, it could be argued that it was only God's pure undeserved grace that allowed these promises to reach fulfillment. If it was predicated solely on with the obedience to conditions, these covenants would never have been fulfilled.

But most of the covenants of God are if-then propositions. When God made a covenant with the people of Israel, He said, "*If* you honor Me, *then* this is what will happen to you." Obedience to the conditions of a covenant is normally crucial to the dispersal of the covenant's blessings and privileges. Above all, the essence of our covenant with God is life. Someone precious gave His life for our freedoms and privileges as joint heirs in the Kingdom. Now it is time for us, as His Body on earth, to justify the cost of God's sacrificial covenant with mankind. We do that by "keeping" covenant with Him through obedience, through constant recognition or remembrance of the covenant, and with lives marked by thankful hearts.

Notes
1. See Genesis 17:19; Galatians 3:16.
2. See Galatians 3:17.
3. Deuteronomy 28:1-10,12.
4. As we noted in Chapter 2, see Galatians 3:13,14; Galatians 4:4-7.
5. John 15:13.
6. The Greek word translated by the authorized *KJV* as "trucebreaker" and by the *NIV* as "unforgiving" is *aspondos*. The word literally means "without libation." In Bible times, truces, treaties and covenants were toasted and sealed with a toast or libation. By implication, this word means "truceless, implacable, a trucebreaker." James Strong, *Strong's Exhaustive Concordance of the Bible* (Peabody, MA: Hendrickson Publishers, n.d.), meanings and definitions drawn from the word derivations for "trucebreakers" (Greek, #786).
7. 2 Timothy 3:1-5.
8. See Proverbs 26:27.
9. I doubt that the United States Navy would use the word "covenant" for it, however.
10. John 15:13.
11. Hebrews 9:15, italics mine.
12. See Jeremiah 31:31-34.

the history of
COVENANT

SECTION TWO

COVENANT
keepers who changed the world

CHAPTER 4

Faithfulness—the Bedrock of Covenant

By now you know that biblical covenant is more than just a written or spoken agreement between two parties. For illustration purposes, let me say that a biblical covenant is 90 percent relationship and only 10 percent documentation. The first covenants were almost totally based on the relationship between God and individual people. The only legal agreements involved in these covenants were the specific promises God made to His covenant partners.

For this reason, we will freely use the word "covenant" to express the faithfulness we demonstrate toward God in our choices and lifestyles. You will also notice that there are many covenant keepers in the Scriptures who never received a specific covenant from God, but instead based their lives on the covenants established before them, much as we do today.

Covenant keepers always reap blessings for their faithfulness and for their faith in God's faithfulness. Some of the covenant keepers of the past played key roles in the purposes and plans of God for all mankind.

Noah was a covenant keeper. In fact, Noah kept covenant with God even though the people of his day had long ago ceased to believe in His existence or had run after other gods. The only spoken covenants in effect were the elementary covenants God spoke over Adam and Eve many centuries earlier concerning their calling to rule and exercise dominion over the earth.

Noah had received a godly inheritance through his great-grandfather, Enoch, and was able to hear the voice of the Lord with great accuracy. For 100 years, he endured the taunts and ridicule of scoffers as he worked on a great boat in a land that was in a long-term drought. As we noted in the second chapter, the Bible says, "Noah was a righteous man, blameless among the people of his time, *and he walked with God*."[1] His faithfulness as a covenant keeper or relationship keeper preserved the human race and key members of the animal kingdom as well.

People in Key Bible Events Were Just That—People!

Too many times we isolate biblical narratives about key figures like Noah and Abraham and treat them as if they are mere stylized fiction or, just as wrongly, as if the individuals involved were superhuman and totally unlike us in every respect. The facts are that these events really happened, and that the people involved were just that: *people*.

The only perfect party to any heavenly covenant is God. Everybody else is covered by His grace.

Noah drank too much wine to celebrate his first grape harvest after the flood and ended up in a real mess with his sons and grandsons. Abraham tried to save his own life by pretending that Sarah was his sister, and a powerful king almost added her to his harem. Then, although Abraham had heard the Lord reassure him that the prophecy about his children would come to pass, he consented to his wife's scheme to help him have a son through her handmaiden.[2]

The point is that God chose to make covenants with real people who were not perfect. The only perfect party to any heavenly covenant is God, and God alone. Everything and everybody else is covered by His grace.

We have already examined the life of Abraham to a certain extent, but there is much more we can learn from his example. One of the most powerful statements God made about Abraham is directly linked to his identity as a true covenant keeper:

Abraham will surely become a great and powerful nation, and all nations on earth will be blessed through him. *For I have chosen him, so that he will direct his children and his household after him to keep the way of the LORD by* doing what is right and just, so that the LORD will bring about for Abraham what he has promised him.[3]

Abraham was chosen by God because the Lord knew He could trust him to train his children to follow in the path of holiness. Abraham had to wait a long time to see the first part of God's promise come to pass, but in due time, Sarah gave birth to Isaac, the son of promise, when Abraham was 100 years old.[4]

Isaac Would Understand Jesus' Covenantal Sacrifice

The Lord allowed Abraham to prove where his heart was anchored with the test of fire on Mount Moriah. In obedience to God's command, Abraham took his young son, Isaac, to Mount Moriah and then bound and placed him on an altar of God. Abraham's son saw God provide a ram in his place and possibly heard the voice of God once again pronounce the blessings of covenant over his father, Abraham, and over himself. If any person in the Old Testament could ever understand the true meaning of the Cross, it would have been Isaac, the man whose life was spared when Jehovah-Jireh (God Will Provide), provided a ram to take his place on the altar of sacrifice.[5]

Isaac had his share of troubles when his wife gave birth to twins, and the two sons remained at odds until late in their life. The elder son, Esau, loved to please his father, but his god was his appetite. The other son, Jacob, was a deceiver and trickster who was destined to be transformed by a personal encounter with God in the midst of his greatest trial.[6]

Jacob stole his elder brother's birthright with a bowl of lentil soup. Then he managed to fool his father, Isaac, into giving him the father's blessing traditionally reserved for the eldest son in the family. This happened in the twilight of Isaac's life, and it was customary that once such blessings were pronounced, they could never be taken back.[7]

Jacob's deceiving ways made things so bad at home that he had to flee for his life to avoid Esau's angry lust for vengeance. This is not a typical picture of a covenant keeper. In fact, at this point in the Bible narrative, it looks like God's covenant with Abraham's descendants is certain to break down. However, we should never forget that God guards His covenants (even when we don't). He will move heaven and earth to preserve covenant when necessary. Just before Jacob left home, his father, Isaac, called him once again and delivered this transgenerational covenant blessing:

> So Isaac called for Jacob and blessed him and com-manded him: "Do not marry a Canaanite woman [like Esau, who married two Hittite women]. Go at once to Paddan Aram, to the house of your mother's father Bethuel. Take a wife for yourself there, from among the daughters of Laban, your mother's brother. May God Almighty bless you and make you fruitful and increase your numbers until you become a community of peo-ples. *May he give you and your descendants the blessing given to Abraham, so that you may take possession of the land where you now live as an alien, the land God gave to Abraham.*"[8]

Jacob lived with his uncle, Laban, and left there after years of labor, married to two of Laban's daughters, with many children and a wealth of livestock and servants. Yet his greatest challenge and a name-changing transformation still awaited him.

Jacob's Change in Name and Destiny

The covenant-keeping God was about to intercept Jacob's life at the river Jabok. Trapped between his father-in-law's territory behind him and Esau's band of armed men in front, Jacob sent his family and goods ahead while he waited alone beside the river. The Bible says a man, perhaps a theophany of Christ, wrestled with Jacob until the sun rose the following morning when Jacob experienced a dramatic change of name and destiny:

> When the man saw that he could not overpower him, he touched the socket of Jacob's hip so that his hip was wrenched as he wrestled with the man. Then the man said, "Let me go, for it is daybreak." But Jacob replied, "I will not let you go unless you bless me." The man asked him, "What is your name?" "Jacob," he answered. Then the man said, *"Your name will no longer be Jacob, but Israel, because you have struggled with God and with men and have overcome."* Jacob said, "Please tell me your name." But he replied, "Why do you ask my name?" Then he blessed him there. So Jacob called the place Peniel, saying, "It is because I saw God face to face, and yet my life was spared."[9]

God intervened in the meandering, deceit-ridden life of Jacob the trickster to preserve His covenant with his grandfather, Abraham. First He planted Jacob in Laban's household where his character was gradually reformed as he was forced to work hard, suffered long-term disappointments, and was mistreated and misled. In the midst of his plans for a final deception of his brother, Esau, God met Jacob and changed his name from Jacob the trickster to Israel, which means "he will rule as God."

After Jacob ordered his sons and their families to turn away from their idols and false gods, the Lord again met Jacob and called him Israel and expanded and extended His covenant with Jacob/Israel:

And God said to him, "I am God Almighty; be fruitful and increase in number. A nation and *a community of nations* will come from you, *and kings will come from your body. The land I gave to Abraham and Isaac I also give to you,* and I will give this land to *your descendants after you*."[10]

In time, Jacob's sons would become the patriarchs of Israel. Joseph, Jacob's younger son, was another covenant keeper who withstood decades of difficulty and adversity in Egypt after his jealous older brothers sold him into slavery. He rose to be the chief ruler of Egypt under the Hyksos Pharaohs, and was gracious and forgiving to his brothers when they were reunited.[11]

It was Joseph who brought his father's entire family from drought-stricken Canaan to Egypt (in fulfillment of God's prophetic covenant with Abraham).[12] There Jacob announced that the two sons born to Joseph in Egypt, Ephraim and Manasseh, would be counted as sons of Jacob (they became the fathers of entire tribes) with the rights and privileges of sons rather than grandsons.[13]

God Fulfilled Joseph's Boyhood Visions

In all of his troubles, Joseph remained a covenant keeper. As a result, the visions God gave him as a boy of 17 came to pass and he helped bring about yet another major portion of God's covenant with Abraham, Isaac and Jacob.[14]

After Joseph and his memory passed from the scene, the descendants of Israel multiplied so much in Egypt that the new Pharaoh of that era began to fear them. He ordered that the Israelites be enslaved, and over the next 400 years, Hebrew slave labor helped build the Egyptian cities of Pithom and Rameses.[15] God heard the cries of the Jews and the Bible says He "remembered His covenant with Abraham, with Isaac and with Jacob."[16] Then the "angel of the Lord" (most likely an epiphany of Christ Himself) called to Moses from within a burning bush and decreed a verbal covenant that established Moses as God's deliverer for the Jews:

> God called to him from within the bush, "Moses! Moses!" And Moses said, "Here I am." "Do not come any closer," God said. "Take off your sandals, for the place where you are standing is holy ground." Then he said, "I am the God of your father, the God of Abraham, the God of Isaac and the God of Jacob." At this, Moses hid his face, because he was afraid to look at God. The LORD said, "I have indeed seen the misery of my people in Egypt. I have heard them crying out because of their slave drivers, and I am concerned about their suffering. So I have come down to rescue them from the hand of the Egyptians and to bring them up out of that land into a good and spacious land, a land flowing with milk and honey—the home of the Canaanites, Hittites, Amorites, Perizzites, Hivites and Jebusites. And now the cry of the Israelites has reached me, and I have seen the way the Egyptians are oppressing them. *So now, go. I am sending you to Pharaoh to bring my people the Israelites out of Egypt.*"[17]

Parroting Moses' Objections to God's Covenant Call

What followed God's announcement should encourage every one of us as covenant keepers. Moses promptly began to produce excuses and arguments to disqualify himself from God's covenant task, but the Lord was determined to complete His plan. Five times Moses presented objections to God's call on his life. These objections are echoed every day by modern day believers whom God is calling to covenant service in His kingdom:

1. First, Moses claimed he wasn't up to the job.
2. Then he said that no one would understand if he said that an invisible God without a name sent him to deliver them from Pharaoh (so God revealed afresh His name to Moses).
3. Moses also claimed that even if people believed in the invisible God, they certainly wouldn't believe "You sent me."
4. He said, "But God, I'm not really a talker or public speaker—I stutter." God answered him by reminding him who made his lips and tongue.
5. Finally, Moses abandoned the excuses and started begging: "Please send someone else." That could be the central theme of the modern Church![18]

One by one, God answered Moses' questions and objections with divine provision until Moses had only one choice left—believe God and keep the covenant, or disbelieve the voice from the burning bush and reject the covenant of God. He does the same for us today.

Moses proved to be perhaps the best covenant keeper in the Old Testament. At the very least, he was the instrument God used to initiate the greatest covenant in the Old Testament at Mount Sinai. Most Christians and Jews think of Mount Sinai as the place where God delivered the Law (the Ten Commandments and over 600 laws) to Moses. Yet much more was going on at Mount Sinai. The Law was but a small part of a much larger covenant that involved the fulfillment of previous covenants, the creation of a new covenant, and the foreshadowing of the greatest blood covenant of all time—the covenant of eternal life and divine fellowship cut by Jesus Christ on the cross of Calvary.

Set Aside to Be the "People of God"

It was at Mount Sinai that God called the now numerous descendants of Abraham, Isaac, and Jacob/Israel out of bondage into a new identity as the "people of God."[19] With the construction of the Tabernacle according to God's instructions, everything about this new nation was to be God centered. In return, God literally came down to dwell among His people, foreshadowing the greater covenant at Calvary when God would dwell in the hearts of His people forever.[20]

Joshua became Moses' personal assistant and companion. He alone accompanied Moses into the presence of God on Mount Sinai, and entered the Tent of Presence with him.[21] He would remain in God's presence long after Moses left. Joshua was a remarkable covenant keeper who was considered faithful enough to carry on Moses' leadership after his death. Joshua's leadership anointing was rooted in his personal relationship with God. With the children of Israel on the verge of crossing the river Jordan into the Promised Land after 40 years of wandering, God extended Moses' covenant to Joshua, with some unique additions and provisions:

> Moses my servant is dead. Now then, you and all these people, get ready to cross the Jordan River into the land I am about to give to them—to the Israelites. I will give you every place where you set your foot, as I promised Moses. *No one will be able to stand up against you all the days*

of your life. As I was with Moses, so I will be with you; I will never leave you nor forsake you. Be strong and courageous, because you will lead these people to inherit the land I swore to their forefathers to give them. Do not let this Book of the Law depart from your mouth; meditate on it day and night, so that you may be careful to do everything written in it. Then you will be prosperous and successful. Have I not commanded you? Be strong and courageous. *Do not be terrified; do not be discouraged, for the LORD your God will be with you wherever you go.*[22]

Faithful Covenant Keepers

Joshua died at the age of 110, and he faithfully kept the covenant of God throughout his lifetime. The Bible says, "Israel served the LORD throughout the lifetime of Joshua and of the elders who outlived him and who had experienced everything the LORD had done for Israel."[23] Joshua the covenant keeper must have done something right to have that kind of statement made about him.

David and Jonathan were covenant keepers in two realms. They not only honored and kept the covenant of God, but they both risked everything to keep their covenant with God and with one another. This is the picture of true covenant keepers.

After David had finished talking with Saul, Jonathan became one in spirit with David, and he loved him as himself. From that day Saul kept David with him and did not let him return to his father's house. And *Jonathan made a covenant with David because he loved him as himself.* Jonathan took off the robe he was wearing and gave it to

David, along with his tunic, and even his sword, his bow and his belt.[24]

Jonathan, the son of King Saul, was heir to his father's throne by all of the customs of men and nations. Yet he demonstrated that his first loyalty was to the God of Israel, not to his father and earthly king. Jonathan was older than David, and long before David came on the national scene, Jonathan had become a national hero with his brave exploits as a soldier, leader and believer in God. He knew firsthand just how dangerous his father could be—at one point in his life, the men of Israel had to intervene to save Jonathan's life after his father made a rash declaration and refused to admit his error.[25]

Jonathan Loved David As He Loved Himself

When Jonathan first met David, his heart was immediately bound to him and they became closer than brothers. As the Scriptures say, "Jonathan made a covenant with David because he loved him as himself."[26] This is yet another picture of the New Testament standard Jesus set for covenant love among the brethren. Jonathan was determined to protect his friend from his father's wrongful anger, even after King Saul threw a spear at his son in his anger when he stood up for David.[27]

Jonathan was a spiritual man who understood that he was involved in a much larger plan of God than most people believed—he even knew David was God's choice to take his place on the throne, and he was determined to make sure it happened:

And Saul's son Jonathan went to David at Horesh and helped him find strength in God. "Don't be afraid," he said. "My father Saul will not lay a hand on you. You will be king over Israel, and I will be second to you. Even my father Saul knows this." The two of them made a covenant before the LORD.[28]

After Jonathan was killed in battle along with his father, King Saul, David ultimately assumed the thrones of Judah and Israel.[29] He made a special effort to keep his covenant with his deceased friend by seeking out his last living male descendant, Mephibosheth. Then he brought him into the palace to live and share the royal family dinner table in the classic Middle Eastern demonstration of covenant trust and relationship: "'Don't be afraid,' David said to him, 'for I will surely show you kindness for the sake of your father Jonathan. I will restore to you all the land that belonged to your grandfather Saul, and you will always eat at my table.'"[30]

God Even Uses Reluctant Covenant Keepers—
If They Are Faithful

There are many more examples of anointed covenant-keepers in the Old Testament, but our examination concludes with Esther, one of the most revered (and reluctant) covenant keepers in ancient Jewish history. Esther grew up as a fatherless child taken in by a covenant keeping cousin, Mordecai. They were Jews who had been carried away from Jerusalem after Israel was conquered by the Babylonian king Nebuchadnezzar many years earlier.[31]

As the drama unfolds, Esther was selected and taken into the king's harem with other virgins when the king began a country-wide search for a queen. King Artaxerxes loved Esther more than all of the other women and named her queen. Meanwhile, Mordecai uncovered a plot to assassinate the king and passed it on to Queen Esther. She told the king, the plotters were executed, and Mordecai's deed was recorded in the king's official annals of history.[32]

Shortly after this, the king elevated a man named Haman to the second-most-powerful position in the kingdom. When Mordecai refused to bow down to or honor Haman, he hatched a secret plot to kill Mordecai and every other Jewish person living in the territories controlled by the king (both he and the king were totally unaware that the king's new queen was Jewish as well).[33]

When Mordecai discovered Haman's secret plot, he put on sackcloth and ashes and could no longer visit Esther in the palace. She sent her servant out to see what was wrong, and Mordecai explained everything. Then he told the servant to "urge her to go into the king's presence to beg for mercy and plead with him for her people."[34] Esther replied with a message explaining that anyone who approached the king without a prior invitation faced an instant death sentence unless the king chose to extend his scepter toward them and spare their lives.

Esther's Reply Should Be Our Reply

Mordecai's reply is a timeless warning to every covenant keeper of God about the importance of obedience and accepting personal responsibility for the welfare of others. Esther's response to her covenant duty is what God expects to hear from each of us where His covenant is concerned:

> Do not think that because you are in the king's house you alone of all the Jews will escape. For *if you remain silent at this time, relief and deliverance for the Jews will arise from another place,* but you and your father's family will perish. And *who knows but that you have come to royal*

position for such a time as this? Then Esther sent this reply to Mordecai: "Go, gather together all the Jews who are in Susa, and fast for me. Do not eat or drink for three days, night or day. I and my maids will fast as you do. *When this is done, I will go to the king, even though it is against the law. And if I perish, I perish.*"[35]

It is clear that the birth of every single covenant keeper in the Old Testament was preordained by God for His divine purposes. Why should it be different for you? God is no respecter of persons,[36] so He brought you into this world for a divine purpose unique to you. The only way to live a fulfilled life in Christ is to live as a covenant keeper, as a person who understands that your life is not your own, for you have been bought with a price by blood covenant.[37]

Once you grasp the vast scope of God's purpose for this generation, and perceive that you have a vital part to play in His plan (whether your life affects the future of one person or 10 million people), you will approach every day of life with a new perspective. Even the casual, everyday duties you perform may take on increased importance as you realize that the steps of your life are ordered by the Lord. He regularly sends covenant keepers out for divine appointments with people every single day. God uses covenant keepers to change the world—are you ready?

Notes
1. Genesis 6:9, italics mine.
2. See Genesis 9:20-27; 12:10-20; 16:1-4.
3. Genesis 18:18,19, italics mine.
4. See Genesis 21:5.
5. See Genesis 22:3-18.
6. See Genesis 25:21-26,29-34; 32:22-32.

7. See Genesis 25:29-34; 27:1-40.
8. Genesis 28:1-4, italics mine.
9. Genesis 32:25-30, italics mine.
10. Genesis 35:11,12, italics mine.
11. See Genesis 37:12-36; 41:39,40; 42—45.
12. See Genesis 15:18; 45:17,18.
13. See Genesis 48:5,6.
14. See Genesis 37:1-11.
15. See Genesis 15:13; Exodus 1:11.
16. See Exodus 2:23-25.
17. Exodus 3:4-10, italics mine.
18. These objections and God's answers can be found respectively in Exodus 3:11,13; 4:1,10,13.
19. See Exodus 3:7; 19:6; 22:31; Leviticus 26:12; Numbers 6:27.
20. See John 1:14; Ephesians 3:17.
21. See Exodus 24:13; 33:11.
22. Joshua 1:2,3,5,6,8,9, italics mine.
23. Joshua 24:31.
24. 1 Samuel 18:1-4, italics mine.
25. 1 Samuel 18:3.
26. See 1 Samuel 14:43-45.
27. 1 Samuel 20:30-33.
28. 1 Samuel 23:16-18.
29. See 2 Samuel 1:4; 2:4; 5:1-3.
30. 2 Samuel 9:7.
31. Esther 2:5-7.
32. Esther 2:1-4,8,17-23.
33. Esther 3:1-11.
34. Esther 4:8.
35. Esther 4:13-16, italics mine.
36. See Acts 10:34.
37. See 1 Corinthians 6:19,20; 7:23.

COVENANT
in the New Testament

CHAPTER 5

Seeing Through the Eyes of Covenant

Many Christians seem to believe that covenant is strictly an Old
Testament concept, and for that reason they feel it isn't worthy
of serious study or application. The truth is that covenant permeates the events, teachings and doctrines of the New
Testament! Nearly all Christians know that covenant is in the
Old Testament, even if they don't have a clear understanding of
it. Now we need to allow the Holy Spirit to teach us about
covenant in the New Testament, or what the Old Testament
looks forward to and what Jesus identified as the New
Covenant.

Jesus Christ, God the Son, came to the earth because of God's covenant with Adam and Eve, Abraham, Isaac and Jacob; Moses, David, Daniel and the people of Israel. He entered the world of man on a covenant-keeping mission, and He came as a baby born into the covenant-based culture and faith of the Jews. He was circumcised on the eighth day in accordance with the covenantal requirements for firstborn males,[1] and he was dedicated to the Lord in the Temple at Jerusalem in strict accordance with Levitical law.[2]

The Lord was born into a covenant-keeping family, and He was raised by Joseph and Mary to be a covenant-keeping, Law-observing Jew. We know from the Scriptures that Jesus grew up studying and observing the tenets of the Abrahamic and Mosaic covenants, and demonstrated such knowledge in these things that He amazed the best Jewish teachers and scribes when He was 12.[3]

Even the genealogies listed in the Gospels contain powerful examples of our covenant-keeping God remembering His promises and covenants to the patriarchs and to key men and women over the preceding centuries!

The Gospels and the book of Acts reveal the rich covenantal relationship Jesus maintained with His disciples. Many people do not realize that in the early period of His adult ministry, Jesus was closer to His disciples than to His own family members.[4]

The reason is simple when we look through the eyes of covenant: When the time came for Jesus Christ to begin His covenant mission and operate in His calling as the Messiah, His earthly family couldn't handle the transition. They kept looking at Jesus through the eyes of the flesh, and all they saw was an elder brother or a son who grew up in their family home. The Bible says, "Even his own brothers did not believe in him."[5]

Jesus could only enter into a covenant relationship with people who needed someone to love them, or who believed He was a miracle worker sent from God, or who were looking for the Messiah to come. Those who were totally self-sufficient and self-absorbed would never do, because those in covenant with Him demonstrated their loyalty by leaving everything to follow Him. Jesus loved His earthly family, but He could not violate His covenant with God the Father for their sakes. He did everything to reclaim them, and in the end His brothers were saved.

Those who entered into covenant with Jesus soon discovered that He was out to extend and expand the ancient covenants of God. He told His disciples in the latter part of His earthly ministry:

> I no longer call you servants, because a servant does not know his master's business. Instead, I have called you friends, for everything that I learned from my Father I have made known to you. You did not choose me, but I chose you and appointed you to go and bear fruit—fruit that will last. Then the Father will give you whatever you ask in my name. This is my command: Love each other.[6]

Covenant Doesn't Differentiate Between Convenience and Inconvenience

Jesus said these things to His disciples on the very night He was to be betrayed. He was saying, "You are My friends because I chose to make you friends. That means you have Me as your friend even in My weakest hour. I will not only visit you at My convenience, but I will also visit you when it is not convenient." That is the essence of true covenant.

The Lord demonstrated true covenant in everything He did. He wasn't interested in the value of mere words; He demonstrated by example that words are only powerful when they are backed up by truth and by true actions. When Jesus called people like Zacchaeus, the chief tax collector, out of a tree, or called Levi directly from his tax collection tables, the moment He entered into covenant with them, He demonstrated it by eating with them.

This kind of truth in action totally offended those Jews who were married to the letter of the Law instead of the spirit. Their words reveal exactly what offended them. We often see the words, "Why do you eat and drink with tax collectors and 'sinners'?"[7]

They were often intrigued by Jesus' authoritative teachings (when they weren't cut to the heart by guilt), but they were nearly always offended by His pure-hearted, nonreligious application of those truths to the dregs of Jewish society. Their offense was even greater because they came from a covenant-based society: They knew that any time a man ate with someone, there was a potential for true covenant.

The Gospels record many instances where Jesus defied accepted social and religious custom to eat with or enter the homes of known sinners. He was called a glutton, drunkard, and friend of tax gatherers and sinners.[8] He associated with morally or religiously unclean people, such as prostitutes or those afflicted with leprosy.[9] Jesus even broke bread with the religious elite if they were truly seeking the truth, but it was during these meals that Jesus was sometimes visited by the lowlife individuals to whom He also extended the high privilege of covenant relationship.

Jesus Christ is the living embodiment of God's covenant with us. The human race as a whole is one great conglomeration of lowlife individuals in desperate need of a savior and deliverer. Jesus loved us first—when we were unlovable—and He personally set us free to love and walk in true covenant.[10]

The Mystery of the Ages Reveals
Our Covenant of Faith

The Lord didn't come to this earth to take advantage of us, or to get us to build His kingdom so He could move on to bigger and better things. As the apostle Paul explains in his epistle to the Ephesians, God sent Jesus Christ to declare and complete the unthinkable, the blood covenant of salvation that is called the "mystery of the ages" in the New Testament:

> And he made known to us the mystery of his will according to his good pleasure, which he purposed in Christ, to be put into effect when the times will have reached their fulfillment—to bring all things in heaven and on earth together under one head, even Christ. *In him we were also chosen*, having been predestined according to the plan of him who works out everything in conformity with the purpose of his will.[11]

In reading this, then, you will be able to understand my insight into the *mystery of Christ*, which was not made known to men in other generations as it has now been revealed by the Spirit to God's holy apostles and prophets. This mystery is that through the gospel the Gentiles are heirs together with Israel, members together of one Body, and sharers together in the promise in Christ Jesus—

> and to make plain to everyone the *administration of this mystery,* which for ages past was kept hidden in God, who created all things. *His intent was that now, through the church, the manifold wisdom of God should be made known to the rulers and authorities in the heavenly realms,* according to his eternal purpose which he accomplished in Christ

Jesus our Lord. In him and through faith in him we may approach God with freedom and confidence.[12]

What Is the Modern Church Really Manifesting to the World?

This divine mystery can only be fulfilled by a Church *that walks in covenant* with God! The modern Church has difficulty in making known "the manifold wisdom of God" when it doesn't understand covenant. It is more likely to present its comfortable traditions rather than submission to one another, unity and covenant living. God is out to change things in His earthly Body.

In the previous passage from Ephesians, Paul begins by reminding us of what God has done and what He says to us in His Word: "You are now My children. Whatever I have is yours and whatever you have is Mine, for you share My kingdom." As always, the Lord gives us far more than He asks of us. Divine covenant has a way of saying, "I am going to give you far more than you will ever be able to give back to Me."

Perhaps the greatest example of the way Jesus extended the privileges of true covenant to people most folks would avoid is found in the life of the prostitute we mentioned in a previous chapter, the woman who brought an expensive alabaster box of fragrant anointing oil or ointment and anointed Jesus for His burial. There is substantial proof in the Bible that this woman was Mary, the sister of Martha and Lazarus. In fact, when you compare the Gospel accounts, it is possible that Mary anointed Jesus *twice*, once earlier in His ministry, and then late in His life, the night Judas betrayed Him.[13]

When Jesus aligned Himself with Mary, Martha and Lazarus, He was publicly cutting a covenant with a dysfunctional family of public record. Since the Bible makes no mention of their parents, they were apparently dead. Neither of the sisters was married, and since the Scriptures clearly indicate that Mary in particular was a "woman who lived a sinful life" in her hometown,[14] it is almost certain that this dysfunctional family was also considered a dishonorable family supported at least in part by the profits of prostitution or immorality until her life changing encounter with Jesus Christ.

Covenant Changed Everything for Mary and Martha

Mary, Martha and Lazarus were all siblings living in a fragmented household on the fringe of society in Bethany. When Lazarus died, all hope was gone for his two sisters. They weren't married, and by Jewish social and religious standards, Mary's known involvement in immorality forever disqualified her for honorable marriage. Covenant changed all of that in God's eyes, because by cutting covenant with this broken and dysfunctional family, Jesus became the head of their household and their hope for the future. He does the same thing for us today with His blood covenant!

When Jesus came into the lives of Mary, Martha and Lazarus, they entered into a relationship that was so deep that they knew Jesus would never destroy the covenant. Many Christians wonder how Mary and Martha could be so demanding or assume so much when they expected Jesus to come to them when Lazarus died. They knew they could call upon Jesus because of their covenant relationship with Him.

Mary and Martha didn't assume anything; they were operating in the relationship Jesus established with them (their only error was in the area of faith). When you have covenant, covenant will put demands on you to meet with and spend time with the people when it is convenient and when it is not con-

venient. Even American customs recognize this kind of obligation when
it comes to a death in the immediate
family. There are times when the responsibilities of preexistent relationships take precedence over everything
else.

If I am in covenant with you, I have
an obligation to get up if you come
and knock on my door in the middle
of the night—and vice versa. On the
other hand, if you abuse that relationship, covenant requires me to tell
you the truth and apply healthy influence to bring your actions into proper
alignment. Covenant involves much
more than a relationship between friends; it is more like a family relationship, and this is what you see throughout the New
Testament.

> Covenant requires me to tell you the truth and apply healthy influence to your actions.

God May Do the Impossible to Uphold a Covenant

The incident with Lazarus reveals another key aspect of our biblical covenant with Christ. Jesus made a point of waiting four
days before He returned to Bethany because He intended to confirm the seriousness of His covenant with Mary, Martha and
Lazarus. He wanted His adopted family—and those like you and
me who would follow later—to know that, in the mind of God,
covenant means that *if He has to do the impossible* in order to honor
His covenant, then He will do it!

Up to that point, healings and miracles were commonplace
in Jesus' ministry, but few had been raised from the dead. Jesus

intended to raise Lazarus from the dead, but He would do it only after His friend's body had begun to decay (after four days in an unrefrigerated tomb without any embalming chemicals to preserve the body). By the time Jesus finally arrived, all hope for Lazarus was gone and the despair Jesus sensed in the others moved Him so deeply that He wept. Yet for our covenant-keeping God, all things are possible. Covenant will make you attempt the impossible, to try things you've never done before; and covenant may make you cry as you've never cried before.

Covenant is a three-dimensional relationship in which all things are revealed in an atmosphere of clarity and truth. The way Jesus dealt with a hurting and angry Martha reveals how our covenant-keeping God deals with what would normally be considered insubordination in His covenant family. By the time Jesus neared Bethany, Martha's hurt and anger were nearly unbearable. She literally began to berate Jesus for taking so long to return. In Jewish society in that day, it wasn't considered acceptable for a woman to berate a rabbi or civic leader. Jesus simply took it with grace and then He gently and privately corrected her and led her the right way. This is covenant relationship at its finest.

The Unconditional Love of Covenant

Martha was clearly out of line, but Jesus knew her heart and He understood her pain. He wasn't worried about His public appearance, His pride or the opinions of onlookers—He was concerned about Martha! He loved this precious woman with the servant's heart. He remembered all of the meals she had prepared for and shared with Him. He hadn't forgotten all of the ways she had labored to honor Him and make Him comfortable in her home. He wasn't about to let the pressures that forced her to go over the line also rob her of the unconditional covenant love she so desperately needed in her hour of need.

As always, Jesus did for Lazarus, Mary and Martha what He always does for those in covenant with Him. He did for them what they couldn't do for Him: He gave them life. Covenant always requires the one who initiates covenant to give more than those who receive the benefits of the covenant.

The covenant of Christ is both vertical and horizontal in the sense that it involves both our relationship to God (the vertical aspect) and our relationship to other people (the horizontal aspect). Christ's covenant makes you kinder and more tolerant of others. It makes you more understanding and more compassionate.

Perhaps you have noticed that people who either do not perceive their covenant in Christ or simply don't have covenant often become judgmental, condemning and even vindictive toward others. Unfortunately, evidence seems to indicate that the Church also is becoming more and more judgmental, condemning and vindictive rather than more gracious in Christ. Paul delivered one of the most graphic warnings about broken covenant in the New Testament when he wrote to the Church in Corinth about holy Communion:

> Therefore, whoever eats the bread or drinks the cup of the Lord in an unworthy manner will be guilty of sinning against the body and blood of the Lord. A man ought to examine himself before he eats of the bread and drinks of the cup. For anyone who eats and drinks *without recognizing the body of the Lord* eats and drinks judgment on himself. *That is why many among you are weak and sick, and a number of you have fallen asleep* [or died]. But if we judged ourselves, we would not come under judgment.[15]

To fail to recognize the Body of the Lord (the Church) is to be blind to the existence of our joint covenant in Christ, and to break that covenant without regard for the consequences of our selfishness. Regretfully, the modern Church has made mistakes in this area, but I believe that God has a marvelous part for the Church to play in restoring what has been damaged!

Covenant Says "I Will Never Betray You"

When people are in covenant, it is common for them to say, "Look, I will not betray you." Why do they say this? It is because covenant is intricately intertwined with trust, faithfulness and integrity. One of the "root promises" behind every covenant is summed up in the words: "I will never betray you." This is what Jesus was saying when He promised His disciples just before He ascended to heaven, "And surely I am with you always, to the very end of the age."[16]

The life of the apostle Paul is a living testimony to the power of covenant in a man's life. When God knocked Saul of Tarsus to the ground in Acts 9, He was separating unto Himself a religious zealot who was also a murderer and a persecutor of the saints. Until that encounter on the road to Damascus, Saul had no regard for the people of God who followed Jesus Christ. He was determined to kill or imprison as many Christians as he could in the name of God and the Jewish Sanhedrin, and he did his job well.

All of that changed the instant God revealed Himself to Saul, temporarily removed his sight, and told him to go to Damascus and wait for further directions. He fasted and prayed for three days while in total darkness as God began to work on a Christian man in Damascus named Ananias.

Covenant Deals with Your Past, Present and Future

Covenant was involved in every aspect of Paul's life from that moment on. Ananias had heard about Saul's exploits as a persecutor of Christians, and he really didn't want to put himself at risk. Outside of covenant, it is natural for us to focus our attention on a person's past history. Biblical covenant, on the other hand, deals with your past, present and future. That is because God Himself accepts the past, believes in the present and hopes for the future. God responded to Ananias's concerns by revealing His covenant purpose for Paul. Then Ananias risked everything to obey God's command:

> But the Lord said to Ananias, "Go! This man is my chosen instrument to carry my name before the Gentiles and their kings and before the people of Israel. I will show him how much he must suffer for my name." Then Ananias went to the house and entered it. Placing his hands on Saul, he said, "Brother Saul, the Lord—Jesus, who appeared to you on the road as you were coming here—has sent me so that you may see again and be filled with the Holy Spirit." Immediately, something like scales fell from Saul's eyes, and he could see again. He got up and was baptized, and after taking some food, he regained his strength. Saul spent several days with the disciples in Damascus. At once he began to preach in the synagogues that Jesus is the Son of God.[17]

Paul was a man who understood covenant. As the former chief prosecutor for the Jewish Sanhedrin in Jerusalem, he knew what it would mean if he openly revealed he had become a Christian. His response was the true action of a determined, no-turning-back covenant keeper. He immediately went directly to the Jewish synagogue in Damascus and declared his loyalty—not merely by giving his testimony, but by boldly preaching the gospel of the resurrected Christ!

It was Ananias's covenant with God that enabled him to take the hand of a murderer and persecutor of Christians and personally introduce him to the church at Damascus. The Bible account is only a few words long, but it implies that Ananias had to go to the disciples at Damascus and say something like, "Look, you guys can hate me, or you may think I am nuts, but let me tell you what the Lord told me about this man, Saul. You may think you know his history, but God said, 'Forget his history.' I also thought the same way about this guy, but God struck down my doubts and commanded me to meet him face-to-face and pray for him."

A Deeper Understanding of Covenant Changes How We Think

If we can learn the lesson Ananias learned in Damascus, if we can begin to understand the depths of God's covenant with us, it will change the way we think as a body of believers. God simply doesn't judge us based on our record—if He did, we would all be guilty as charged. He chooses to judge us by His blood covenant. In other words, He judges us by His record. That is why the Church has no right or authority to be vindictive towards people who sin or fail in life. We are to be like God and hope for the future based on the reality of our covenant of grace and mercy in Christ.

It was covenant that inspired the apostle Paul to correct the apostle Peter on the matter of race-based favoritism in the Church.[18] Paul knew about the vision Peter had received directly from God declaring that the covenant of salvation through Christ was as powerful and genuine for non-Jewish people (Gentiles) as for Jews.[19] Some time had passed and Peter began to waver on that covenant truth. It was time for a covenant brother to bring correction in the spirit of love, and Paul did the job.

Covenant was even revealed in Peter's actions the time he received the heavenly vision concerning salvation for the Gentiles. When non-Jewish messengers arrived from the Roman centurion, Cornelius, Peter immediately invited them into the house in violation of Jewish custom. Then he went with them and entered the non-Jewish home of Cornelius and ministered the gospel to them.

Peter—You Ate with Gentiles!

Peter did something else there that earned him the criticism of race-conscious Jewish Christians in Jerusalem who complained, "You went into the house of uncircumcised men and ate with them."[20] As we've noted before, the privilege of eating together is intended to bring people into true covenantal relationships. That is why this came up among Peter's Jewish brethren in Jerusalem.

God sent both Peter and Paul to Gentiles—people who were not considered by some Jewish believers to be children of the covenant of Christ unless they also followed Jewish traditions. The Church and the Holy Spirit said that Gentiles did not have to follow all the Jewish customs to be fully included in the New Covenant in Christ's blood. God is still today reaching out to those who are outside the covenant "walls" of the Church!

Covenant is also revealed in the way Christians endured persecution and suffering together in the New Testament. Paul and Barnabas spent time together ministering the gospel in solid covenant love and faithfulness in the face of dangerous opposition. Paul and Silas shared a prison cell together in covenant unity as did Peter and John.[21]

We also see the bonds of covenant at work even in the midst of disagreement between Paul and Barnabas. They had a sharp disagreement over whether or not John Mark could be trusted on a mission trip after he failed on an earlier trip. Paul refused to take him along, so the two men decided to go separate ways.[22] Yet when Paul reached the end of his life and ministry during one of his most difficult times of persecution, it was John Mark who proved himself faithful to the end.[23]

Evidently, Barnabas and John Mark didn't give up on Paul, and Paul didn't give up on them. Somehow, through the bonds of eternal covenant in Christ, John Mark was reunited with Paul the apostle and became his trusted assistant in troubled times. What a testimony of covenant relationship!

We see the bonds of covenant expanding throughout the early life of the Church. Paul urged his young protégé, Timothy, to purposely expand covenant among the ranks of leadership when he said, "And the things you have heard me say in the presence of many witnesses entrust to reliable men who will also be qualified to teach others."[24]

Perhaps we can understand now why many scholars prefer to call the New Testament the "New Covenant" of God. Covenant is at the heart and soul of God's plan of redemption; of the life, ministry, death and resurrection of Christ; and of God's divine purpose for the Church.

Notes
  1. See Luke 2:21.
  2. See Luke 2:22-24; also Exodus 13:2; Leviticus 5:11; 12:6-8.
  3. See Luke 2:40-47.
  4. See Matthew 12:46-49; Mark 3:32-35.
  5. John 7:5.
  6. John 15:15-17.

7. Luke 5:30.

8. See Matthew 11:19.

9. See Matthew 26:6-13; Mark 14:3-9; Luke 7:36-56.

10. See 1 John 4:10,19.

11. Ephesians 1:9-11, italics mine.

12. Ephesians 3: 9-12, italics mine.

13. For more information about Mary and the two times she possibly anointed Jesus with pure oil of nard from an alabaster box or jar, see the following references in the New Testament: Matthew 26:6-13 (takes place in Bethany, at the house of Simon the Leper); Mark 14:3-9 also records the events at the house of Simon the Leper; Luke 7:36-50 possibly describes a different and earlier instance in which a "woman who lived a sinful life in that town" enters a Pharisee's house, wets Jesus' feet with her tears, and wipes them clean with her hair before anointing them with perfume from an alabaster jar. Jesus responds by forgiving her sins; John 11:1,2 clearly identifies Mary as the person who anointed Jesus' feet and wiped them with her hair; John 12:1-8 specifically says that Mary anointed Jesus' feet and head with pure nard, and Jesus rebukes Judas for his disapproval. Then the Lord says Mary was anointing Him for His burial—an exact duplicate of the other gospel.

14. Luke 7:37.

15. 1 Corinthians 11:27-31, italics mine.

16. Matthew 28:20.

17. Acts 9:15-20.

18. See Galatians 2:11-21.

19. See Acts 10.

20. Acts 11:3.

21. See Acts 4:3-23; 13:42-14:23; 16:22,23; 2 Corinthians 11:23-27.

22. See Acts 15:37-39.

23. See 2 Timothy 4:11.

24. 2 Timothy 2:2.

the benefits of
COVENANT

SECTION THREE

power, witness and wealth are
CONSOLIDATED

CHAPTER 6

The Far-Reaching and Long-Term
Effects of Covenant

Myopia is a common vision problem afflicting a large percentage of the human race. Better known as nearsightedness, this condition prevents the human eye from focusing on distant objects. If this condition is left uncorrected, the sufferer is limited to focusing solely on things that are nearby or close up. Everything beyond their limited scope of perception is blurry and indistinct.

Any generation, nation, local church body or family that attempts to exist apart from covenant is almost certainly suffering from myopia of a different sort. It takes the form of generational nearsightedness that threatens to turn all of their focus and attention toward "the now," the present, while leaving the destiny of future generations blurry, fuzzy, indistinct and, therefore, virtually irrelevant.

In other words, apart from covenant, men, churches and nations tend to focus on life today while giving no thought to how present actions and decisions will affect the children, grandchildren and great-grandchildren of tomorrow.

One of the unique qualities of biblical covenant is its ability to transfer and exponentially multiply its benefits to future generations. Jonathan, the son of King Saul, knew this. He also knew or sensed in his spirit that unless something intervened, his father's sins against God and David (God's chosen successor to Saul) would cause the destruction of Saul's family line. That included Jonathan and his descendants.

Jonathan knew there was a solution available if he could find one covenant keeper who was trustworthy. He found that covenant partner in David, his friend who was closer than a brother. When David needed confirmation that Saul intended to kill him, Jonathan agreed to discover the truth, but asked David to make a unique covenant concerning his family line:

Then Jonathan said to David: "By the LORD, the God of Israel, I will surely sound out my father by this time the day after tomorrow! If he is favorably disposed toward you, will I not send you word and let you know? But if my father is inclined to harm you, may the LORD deal with me, be it ever so severely, if I do not let you know and send you away safely. May the LORD be with you as he has been with my father. *But show me unfailing kindness like that of the LORD as long as I live, so that I may not be killed, and do not ever cut off your kindness from my family—not even when the LORD has cut off every one of David's enemies from the face of the earth."* So Jonathan made a covenant with the house of David, saying, *"May the LORD call David's enemies to account."* And Jonathan had David reaffirm his oath out of love for him, because he loved him as he loved himself.[1]

God's Covenants Carry Over to Multiple Generations

The covenant in this passage of Scripture is a *transgenerational* covenant. God intends for all of His covenants to carry over to multiple generations (and He expects ours to do so as well). Although God deals with us individually, He always does so with succeeding generations and eternity in mind. When He works a miracle or answers a prayer in our life today, He does so knowing and expecting that it will affect the lives of family members five years from now and its impact may affect our descendants "to the thousandth generation" of those that love Him.[2] Only God knows the details, but we can count on the fact that everything God does today is meant to have an impact tomorrow and in the years to come.

The time came when Saul and Jonathan lost their lives while fighting with the Philistines, and David was devastated. Saul's last living son, Ish-Bosheth, assumed the throne of all the tribes of Israel except for Judah, which was loyal to David. He ruled Israel for two years until he was assassinated by two brothers from the tribe of Benjamin.[3]

When David finally assumed the throne of Israel, he *remembered his covenant with Jonathan* and personally took the initiative to seek out any living male descendants. He discovered that the curse on Saul's house had already found its way into Jonathan's house as well.[4]

The day a messenger arrived with the news that King Saul and Jonathan had fallen in battle, the nurse who was caring for Jonathan's five-year-old son, Mephibosheth, picked him up to flee but he fell down in their haste. As a result, both of Mephibosheth's feet were so severely damaged that he could no longer walk.[5] David finally located Jonathan's son and last living male heir and asked that he be brought to him:

> When Mephibosheth son of Jonathan, the son of Saul, came to David, he bowed down to pay him honor. David said, "Mephibosheth!" "Your servant," he replied. "Don't be afraid," David said to him, "for *I will surely show you kindness for the sake of your father Jonathan. I will restore to you all the land that belonged to your grandfather Saul, and you will always eat at my table.*"[6]

David fulfilled his covenant with Jonathan in three key ways characteristic of biblical covenants:

1. Although he was now the king, and entitled to vengeance on Saul's family according to the customs of kings in that era (but not according to the ways of God), King David promised to show kindness to Mephibosheth for the sake of his father, Jonathan. This was purely a covenant act since Mephibosheth was the last male in Saul's family line.
2. David promised to *restore* not only Jonathan's land to Mephibosheth, but to restore all of the lands *owned by his grandfather, King Saul*. Then David commanded an entire family who had once served King Saul to now serve Mephibosheth by farming and tending the land and property so that Mephibosheth would have an

independent source of income and a royal inheritance to pass on to his sons.[7]

3. King David demonstrated true covenant by extending to Jonathan's son all of the covenant rights and privileges of his own sons when he promised Mephibosheth he would always eat at the king's table.[8]

Jesus Also Guarantees That We Will Always Dine at His Table

This covenant-keeping act by David foreshadows what Jesus, the Son of David, would do for us. He shows kindness, grace and mercy to us even though by birth we are the sons and daughters of the adversary.[9] He restores to us the privileges, relationship rights and goods stolen from us in the Garden of Eden; and best of all, He guarantees us that we will always dine at the King's table as adopted sons and daughters! Again, we see how true covenant is at the very heart of God's purposes for us today.[10]

The Old Testament has many other examples of how covenants affect future generations. Every human being was affected when Adam and Eve broke their covenant relationship with God in the Garden of Eden. Their sin literally placed us all under the curse of physical and spiritual death.[11]

In the Old Testament, often the sins of the fathers brought negative consequences upon multiple generations in their families. Under the New Covenant of Christ's blood, the curses of past sins by family members can be totally broken.[12] Although the individual may not have the financial power, godly wisdom, and the depth of witness and blessing that comes when many generations in a family follow God faithfully, he can, at the very least, start over as a new creature because of what Christ did on the cross.

We have also benefited from God's unconditional covenantal promise to Eve that her seed would bruise Satan's head—Jesus is the fulfillment of that promise.[13]

The Covenant Kept Growing Stronger with Each Generation

Abraham's patriarchal family is a wonderful example of the power of covenant in godly families. God chose Abraham because the patriarch could be trusted to pass along to his children all of God's revealed truths. The Lord says:

> For I know him, that he will command his children and his household after him, and they shall keep the way of the LORD, to do justice and judgment; that the LORD may bring upon Abraham that which he hath spoken of him.[14]

Despite significant problems, obstacles and calamities along the way, Abraham managed to see his covenant heritage pass along through three generations and beyond. With each generation, the power, breadth and depth of the covenant (and its fulfillment) grew stronger and more far-reaching. This is the way it should be in every God-centered covenant family.

The power of the covenant seemed to reach its first pinnacle after Abraham's descendants spent 400 years in Egypt and God sent Moses to deliverer them exactly as He promised.[15] He caused the descendants of Abraham to leave Egypt wealthier than they were when their ancestors first came there 430 years earlier! A total of 66 members of Jacob's family joined Joseph's family in Egypt for a total of 70 descendants. When they finally left Egypt, the Bible says there were "six hundred thousand men on foot, besides women and children."[16]

Since Moses was a covenant keeper, God extended the covenant of Abraham, Isaac and Jacob/Israel to the Israelites through Moses, and then He expanded it. This new covenant, given through Moses, included details on how the new nation would be governed, what its rules were, and how it would worship, so that the Israelites would be separate from other nations and marked as God's people.

During the period when Israel was crossing the wilderness to enter the Promised Land, God faced the task of teaching a group of former slaves and captives who had been assimilated into Egyptian society how to change their perspective.

Now the Israelites were a nation, not merely a group of related people suffering under the same bondage. Together they experienced God's miraculous deliverance from Pharaoh. Together they saw the cloud of His glory descend on a mountaintop. They awoke each morning to follow His cloud by day and His pillar of fire by night. Their lives were no longer centered on survival as slaves or outcasts in a foreign land—their focus was to be upon the Lord Jehovah, the God who delivered them from bondage and was leading them to their own land.[17]

God Seeks a People Set Apart for Himself

In Moses' day, God provided a sacrificial system, a legal system and a code of holiness (the laws concerning what was clean and unclean); He also provided divine provision and blessing to His people to help them become one people, one nation under God. Through Christ, God provided one final blood sacrifice and a covenant of grace, divine provision and blessing to His people for the same reason—to help us become one people, one holy nation, one Church under God. Consider the following passages from the *NIV*:

You are to be my holy people (Exod. 22:31).

Therefore, as God's chosen people, holy and dearly loved, clothe yourselves with compassion, kindness, humility, gentleness and patience (Col. 3:12).

But you are a chosen people, a royal priesthood, a holy nation, a people belonging to God, that you may declare the praises of him who called you out of darkness into his wonderful light (1 Pet. 2:9).

It all comes back to covenant and the power of covenant to consolidate our power, witness and wealth for His purposes.

When God blessed Abraham, He was also blessing the millions of people who would become his descendants through Isaac. He was also blessing the people from all of the races and nations who would be delivered through Abraham's seed in Christ Jesus. The Lord wasn't merely "waxing eloquent" when He spoke of Abraham's descendants being as numerous as the stars in the heavens. He fully expected His covenant to cause exponential growth in numbers of people, wealth, spiritual and even earthly power. What He said came to pass—despite the failures and faults of the people involved.

The Bible plainly says Jesus is the mediator of a better covenant based on better promises.[18] *Why shouldn't we expect to see an exponential expansion of power, witness and wealth in our lives and especially in the lives of our children, grandchildren and great-grandchildren after us?* There is no reason why this shouldn't happen—unless we fail to recognize the importance of our covenant in Christ and also fail to pass on to our children all of the things we have received and learned from God and from those who went before us.

God Honors Covenantal Prayers
and Keeps His Commitments

When your entire family (including aunts, uncles, grandparents, great-grandparents, etc.) begins to focus on the fundamentals of covenant relationship, your children and grandchildren in the family are empowered to succeed, even where you or those before you have failed. Perhaps you have seen cases where sons went astray in a family, but their grandmother or mother had maintained their covenant with God. They faithfully committed their children and grandchildren to Him, and prayed in faith that He would keep that which they committed unto Him. In due time, whether 1 year or 20 years passed, God honored those covenantal prayers offered in Jesus' name and miraculously restored those young men to the Kingdom.

Covenant is about family, whether it is a physical family or a local family of faith where you worship and serve God. By God's grace, my duties in life span two nations and two cultures. I pastor a local church and maintain an international ministry based in North Carolina. I also have duties as King of Progress and Development for the Shai State in my native land of Ghana.

I see the power of covenant at work every day when I am in Africa. There are many people from Ghana who went to America, mainland Europe, or England to attend top-notch universities. These people often come up to me and say, "Dr. Kingsley Fletcher, your father made it all happen for me. He saw me as a little boy working in the market in our hometown, and he called me aside and said, 'Young man, you have real potential and I feel I should help you.' So your father sent me to school. Every semester he made sure my school fees were paid, and that I had money to go abroad. Now I have come back to return his service to me. I am looking for his children so that I may help them."

It Pays to Invest in the Next Generation

This is a part of our culture in Ghana. Even more, it is a part of all covenantal cultures. We see the same pattern in Jewish communities around the world. An uncle, cousin, grandfather or older brother will sponsor a young man and help him get an education or start a business with an interest-free loan or an outright gift. Yet the unspoken agreement is once they get on their feet and begin to prosper, that young man is to do the same thing with a younger sibling or family member. The wealth of the family and community is always invested back into the next generation and those yet to come.

Giving back is covenant. That includes giving to those who are unable to give back to you. The Bible says, "If a man shuts his ears to the cry of the poor, he too will cry out and not be answered" and "He who gives to the poor will lack nothing, but he who closes his eyes to them receives many curses."[19]

The witness aspect of covenant has to do with our ability to demonstrate true godliness and model the blessings of God before the non-Christians in our communities and nation. We do this to honor God and draw them close to Him, not to show how righteous we are or how unrighteous they are. All of us in the Kingdom are sinners saved by grace. Finger-pointing and hypocrisy are not considered Kingdom skills. They are the stock and trade of Satan, not of Christ the King.

God blesses and prospers His covenant people in Christ for the same reason He blessed the descendants of Abraham. As He declared in His Word:

> The LORD did not set his affection on you and choose you because you were more numerous than other peoples, for you were the fewest of all peoples. But *it was because the LORD loved you and kept the oath he swore to your forefathers* that

he brought you out with a mighty hand and redeemed you from the land of slavery, from the power of Pharaoh king of Egypt. *Know therefore that the LORD your God is God; he is the faithful God, keeping his covenant of love to a thousand generations of those who love him and keep his commands.*[20]

One of the things that we learn in Africa is that we always go back so we can return to society and our family what they have given to us. Virtually all of us know that others have worked to contribute to our welfare and development, even though we may have been raised in the best possible manner by the most exemplary of parents.

The principle is simple: Once you begin to prosper, you go back to bless those who blessed you. If you don't do it for them, then you do it for their children or their children's children. My friend, covenant is catching. There is power in God's plan for covenant living. God has richly blessed me over the years, and He has led many fathers and their sons to help me in my developmental stages of life. Now it has been my privilege to sponsor many of their children so they could go to school. It isn't a burden; it is a blessing. And it is covenant.

Each Generation Accumulates Wisdom, Knowledge and Wealth

The benefits of covenant are especially visible in the areas of resources and business. No matter what we do in life, we need the components of wisdom, knowledge and basic resources to succeed. The wisdom and knowledge are necessary to develop a business plan for both the present and the future. The resources—financial, material or the pool of human skills, talents and abilities—are indispensable in any endeavor.

Covenant encompasses all of these things. Covenant provides the means of passing down the accumulated wisdom and knowledge of our elders to the generations to come. Why should each generation start over at grade one in the area of finances, business management, ministry, agriculture or livestock management?

If God has prospered your family in the area of business management and ownership, isn't it logical that your son, and his son after him, have the opportunity to step into the family business armed with all of the experience, skills and knowledge you have accumulated over your lifetime? That pool of knowledge and wisdom adds up to a tremendous business advantage, doesn't it? This is just a simple example of the exponential power of covenant in our families.

Covenant leaps across the abyss of the unknown into the future and gives hope to the seed or offspring of today's godly covenant keepers. The principles of covenant rest and rely on the even greater spiritual laws of sowing and reaping. That seed of righteousness, faith, generosity or hope that you sow today may well produce the abundant harvest that will feed, clothe, educate and propel your grandchildren into their destiny 50 years from now!

I can tell you that I have benefited from covenant in my life. Whether it was the covenant of love that brought missionaries to Ghana from the West, or the covenant of my father who made

> Covenant provides the means of passing down the accumulated wisdom and knowledge of our elders.

the decision that his house would follow the Lord—I am a beneficiary, and in a good sense, I am a debtor. It is my delight and my duty to sow the seed of covenant back into my family, my parents, my church, and both of the nations I call home today.

The consolidation power of covenant functions a lot like a savings account. It works and compounds value when you put something into it. However, if you open a savings account and simply wait around to receive the interest without ever putting deposits into that account, there will be no interest coming to you. Covenant requires the investment of time, effort, energy, attention and service, whether it is convenient or not. However, its payout is continuous, and according to God's Word, it keeps compounding exponentially to a thousand generations!

Daddy, I Wish You Could Still Discipline Me

I am grateful for the wealth of wisdom and knowledge my father passed down to me from my earliest years. I am a grown man with children of my own, but I like to go back and take my father's hands and tell him, "Hi Daddy. How I have missed your presence in my life. I wish your hands had the strength they once had to put wisdom back into me through your parental correction. Daddy, how I wish you could still discipline me, because I feel that as long as you continue to live on this earth, there is more for me to learn from you."

In a very real sense, our parents and elders pass down the baton of covenant to us when they correct, instruct, lead and invest their time in us as children and young adults. In a covenant-based society like the Church, it should be politically correct to want to be like your father. Above all, the one thing you never want to lose is the blessing and approval of a godly father.

In Ghana, where covenant has been a way of life for centuries (both within and outside of biblical Christianity), the worst thing you can hear your father say is "I will disown you." That means he is saying, "I am cutting the power of covenant in your life, and you will miss out on it." Most of the people in Ghana and many other African and Middle Eastern nations would literally rather die than know they will be disowned by their fathers.

Why is a father's approval so important in the context of covenant? The recognition of the father represents the continuity of history. This concept has been lost in most industrialized nations because of the disintegration and separation of the extended family unit, but every one of us in my family can tell you the history and accomplishments of our fathers to the third or fourth generation. "My father was this, my grandfather was this, my great-grandfather was this, and his father before him was this."

God Knows We Need Continuity

Covenant maintains the unbroken line or thread of inheritance from generation to generation. The God who made us knows that we need continuity in both the natural and the spiritual realms. He is the Rock of our salvation for eternity, and through the bonds of covenant, He ordained that we also have a firm foundation in our family lines as well (both our natural and church families).

As we will see in a later chapter, the Lord also gave us a way to fill the gap where fathers have been lost or simply removed themselves from our lives. He gives us adoptive fathers in the Spirit who share with us their own spiritual stores of wisdom, knowledge, strength, nurture and covenantal power (the apostle Paul did this for Timothy and many other young men).

In Covenant, the Passage Through
Death Is a Family Affair

People who approach death without the peace of the gospel and the framework of biblical covenant are like trees without roots who are caught in a violent wind. They have no ability to stand. They tend to panic because they have no roots that transcend the veil of life, death and eternity.

When your family is covenant oriented, your roots sink deep into the spiritual bedrock of not only Christ but also of multiple generations that have already crossed over by faith into the presence of God. The blood covenant of Christ allows you to know where you are going, so you face death with grace and greater confidence. But you also have greater peace because you know that your going home is a family affair. The covenant commitments that bind family and friends together continue unbroken and unabated right up to the grave, and the bonds of the Spirit pass beyond the grave to eternity in Christ. This powerful bond and strength in covenant love has been largely forgotten today. It is yet another way that covenant consolidates the power and effectiveness of our lives.

After death comes and the living return to the tasks of life, covenant causes them to major on the positive and minor on the negative in their memories of those who have gone on. When the nine children in my father's family gather together in Ghana or in the United States, we don't talk about the negative things that we've been through or the failures of family members who have passed on in death. There are simply too many wonderful memories from their lives and uplifting stories and examples to share from their experiences that will equip and empower us to aim higher in our own lives.

This covenant life is catching, because it is God's gift to enrich our lives here on earth while we await an even greater family reunion in heaven.

Notes
1. 1 Samuel 20:12-17, italics mine.
2. See Exodus 20:6.
3. See 2 Samuel 2:10; 4:5-7.
4. See 2 Samuel 9:1.
5. See 2 Samuel 4:4.
6. 2 Samuel 9:6,7, italics mine.
7. See 2 Samuel 9:9-12.
8. See 2 Samuel 9:9-13.
9. See Ephesians 2:1,2.
10. See Colossians 1:13,14; Revelation 3:20; 19:9.
11. See Genesis 3:1-8; Ezekiel 18:4,20; Romans 5:17.
12. See Galatians 3:13,14; 1 John 1:7.
13. See Genesis 3:15; Romans 16:20.
14. Genesis 18:19, *KJV*.
15. See Genesis 15:13.
16. Exodus 12:37.
17. See Exodus 12—14; 24:16.
18. See Hebrews 8:6.
19. Proverbs 21:13, 28:27.
20. Deuteronomy 7:7-9, italics mine.

families are
FORTIFIED

CHAPTER 7

Covenant Preserves Home
and Anchors Marriage

Covenant is crucial to the well-being of our families and marriages, but most of us find it easy to forget its importance until little reminders intrude into our daily routines. My reminder came in the form of my daughter, Anna-Kissel, who came to my wife, Martha, and me while we were talking. After she joined our conversation, Kissel said to me in a serious tone and depth that went far beyond her youthful age, "Daddy, I know you would never divorce Mommy, because if you did, there would not be any reason for me to live."

I knew my beautiful daughter was trying to communicate to me in a tactful and respectful way, "Daddy, just as you have taught us, we don't welcome dysfunctional relationships in this house. We don't believe it is going to be part of our lives. I trust you to protect us from this kind of danger, no matter how high the cost."

I looked at my daughter and at my beloved wife and said, "Kissel, Daddy is so much in love with Mommy that even if she would ever leave Daddy, then I would go with her. I would follow her to preserve our love and marriage. If I would leave her, then she would follow me as well. Now that issue is settled."

After nearly two decades of marriage, my wife and I are not naive enough to claim we would never encounter opportunities to disagree or feel irritation with one another. Any genuine marriage will include earnest discussions and occasional rough spots in the relationship. But prior to all these marital challenges (for richer or poorer, in sickness and health, etc.) there is an inviolable commitment. On this basis we are confident that our marriage is based upon a lifelong covenant that is sealed in Christ's blood.

My wife and I made a covenant before God. No matter how difficult the road may become, we simply have no option but to walk that road together. We will not even dignify the option of divorce—our commitment to one another is for life. This kind of concrete, covenantal commitment to marriage and family gives our children hope and helps prepare them for the future. My children know that the only way my wife or I will leave our home without the other is by responding to God's eternal call. Only death will part us, and even then it will have a fight on its hands.

How Do We Create and Maintain Covenant in the Home?

Many times in my travels, people will approach me with desperate looks on their faces to ask how they can create covenant in their home. No one has to tell them they have problems—they live with them everyday. They want solutions that work.

Let me ask you this: What do you remember most fondly about your childhood? Take a moment right now, put this book down, and take a mental snapshot of one or two of those wonderful childhood moments. Can you remember all of the toys your parents bought you Christmas after Christmas and on all of those birthdays? Most people can only remember one or two favorite toys. How about all of the trips to your favorite amusement parks, movie theaters or playgrounds? Most people can't remember all of the trips. Rather, they tend to remember isolated incidents that stand out in their memory.

When my brothers and sisters and I sit with our parents, we don't really talk about all of the places our parents took us. We went to many places together and, yes, we enjoyed those times. We also appreciated the things our parents bought for us, because we knew they represented our parents' concern and love for us. What we really love to remember and share together are the simple things Daddy and Mommy taught us to do.

"Daddy, do you remember how you taught me how to lace my shoe?" "Mommy, do you remember when you taught me how to read?" "How about the time you taught me how to tie a knot, Daddy?" One of my personal favorites goes like this: "Daddy, do you remember how we traveled in the car one evening, and you suddenly stopped in the middle of the road and you asked me to go out and smell the air? You wanted me to learn the difference between the smell of the village and the smell of town. Do you remember? I can still hear the sound of the crickets, and how you told me stories that day."

This kind of intimate interchange is how we transfer covenant to our children. It happens every time we make the effort to tell a personal story or paint a word picture for our children that they won't forget. It is the responsibility of parents to create an atmosphere for their children to appreciate covenant. This often involves setting specific boundaries: "This is not part of our family, because our family doesn't do things like that. Yes, others may do it, but not in this house."

The Atmosphere of Home Is the Soil of the Soul

As parents, we must create and control the atmosphere in our homes—not society, not the schools, and not the entertainment, music and news media. The atmosphere of our homes serves as the soil for our children's souls. Covenant helps us create and preserve our identity as people bonded together by shared blood, convictions, heritage, faith and standards of right and wrong. Our children may not like the boundaries we set at times, but without them their future can be destroyed. My father was a disciplinarian who corrected us and punished us when necessary, but he did it fairly. Had he not done so, I wouldn't be where I am today.

It is my conviction that God is at work in the Church in North America, helping us rediscover what "family" truly is. Many of us have condensed our definition of family to "a single living unit consisting of a husband and wife and their children." The biblical examples in both the Old and New Testaments go beyond the husband, wife and children to include grandparents, aunts, uncles, nephews, nieces, great-grandparents, and great-aunts and great-uncles as well. Sometimes it even includes anyone who shows up for dinner on a regular basis.

Roots Give Stability and Strength

Some readers may think I am painting a picture of family life that is too idealistic. Big extended families are a reality in Ghana, just as they were in America 150 years ago. You may still find deep family ties in rural America where there is a strong sense of common traditions, family roots and community. However, in modern urban or suburban industrialized nations, Westerners may have little or no grasp of their own family history or the larger society. Many Westerners barely know their grandparents, let alone their great-grandparents. The past storehouse of wisdom and stories found in one's family history, community past, and culture roots is lost.

There are many factors in industrialized nations today that weaken family connection and community (see chapter 9). A few of the negative forces that come to mind include:

- *Rampant Divorce*—when spouses split up, the children may face an enormous strain on maintaining connection with relatives on a particular side of the family.
- *Working Conditions*—some careers may be so time-consuming as to interfere with a person's desire or ability to meet with other family members.
- *Geographic Distance*—although the Internet is helping to connect family members that live in vastly different areas of the country, vast distances still weaken family bonds. There is no equivalent to physically gathering together the generations and extended parts of a family for picnics and reunions. Children gain an appreciation of their family identity and emotional equilibrium in seeing so many other family members connected.

The Church must invest in a massive repair project to encourage and preserve family heritage in America. The critical keystone is the nature of covenant. So how do you build or rebuild family covenants over generations?

1. *Start with God and His promises of a godly heritage* (see Ps. 127:3). God has saved you for a purpose, and He wants to preserve your family. He wants to bless your family and your generations, within the context of the wider "people of God" through history. Realize that it is by faith, and not by mere human descent, that you have become part of the fulfillment of God's promise to Abraham (see Matt. 3:9); "In other words, it is not the natural children who are God's children, but it is the children of the promise who are regarded as Abraham's offspring" (Rom. 9:8). Also, it is by faith you and your family are called to be lifelong disciples of Christ, and that God takes great delight in you. In fact, the Bible says that "the LORD's portion is his people, Jacob his allotted inheritance" (Deut. 32:9). This means that God's inheritance, what He looks forward to being united with more than anything else, is us, God's own people, created in Christ Jesus for His glory! What an amazing privilege!

2. *Ask God to show you how to be a covenant person and how to create covenant relationships.* God has not forsaken those whose family relationships are very poor or nonexistent; He has promised to be the Father of orphans and widows (see Ps. 68:5), so trust Him to show you how to rebuild.

3. *Gather memories by researching and interviewing family members.* You can accumulate a wonderful background of information (include both tragedies and celebrations, failures and successes, emotional low points and highpoints, etc.) by finding newspaper clippings, photos, and by getting interviews on cassette or videotape.

4. *Begin creating a surrogate extended family* (see the book of Ruth). Make friendships in your church with people who really love Jesus. Among the friends you make,

start looking for covenant friendships—in other words, friendships for life. Don't just look for covenant friendships among people of your own age and situation; spread it out among the generations. Find good friends for your kids, but also try to discover some "grandfathers" and "grandmothers," "uncles" and "aunts" who can share their life experiences and wisdom. See what you can learn from others about mistakes to avoid through life and insights to follow daily.

It Takes More than a Village

The Bible pictures a family as a major league team instead of two loners struggling to raise their family alone. By the time you add the local church family to the mix, you have God's winning team for raising kids, building strong marriages and confirming God's covenant before the world. Outside of covenant, however, you may be left with one or two weary isolated parents struggling to raise their family without the loving support of a covenant church family.

Virtually every relationship in the family and in the Church is rooted in covenant. Covenant relationships are not one-way, nor are they shallow, temporary, part-time or haphazard. For instance, many parents believe their parental role begins and ends with instruction. Yes, our children need instruction, but they need more than instruction—as the apostle Paul said, they need fathers (and mothers) to *imitate*:

Even though you have ten thousand guardians [teachers] in Christ, you do not have many fathers, for in Christ Jesus I became your father through the gospel. Therefore I urge you to imitate me.[1]

We can teach our children how to fish or swim, and we can teach them how to drive, open a bank account, pick out a wardrobe, or even how to conduct themselves in courtship. Yet that in and of itself does not make us good fathers or mothers.

A Good Father Teaches the Difference Between Riches and Wealth

If you will allow me, I will talk a bit more about being a father. A good father is more than a good man; a good father truly *fathers* his children. A good father differentiates between riches and wealth and prepares his child to understand the difference between the two. He will say, "I am going to give you wealth, and this is more valuable and precious than any riches that I could ever give you. Riches can fade away, be stolen or be lost in an instant; but the wealth I am going to give you is an *inheritance*. I want you to know that I am not leaving this inheritance of wealth just for you—I want your children's children to benefit from it as well."

Those who are wise understand that an inheritance of wealth from a father—meaning his wisdom garnered from his life experience, from the successes and failures of multiple generations of fathers—this kind of true wealth can easily produce money and property. More importantly, it produces generations of mature adults who can rule over money and possessions instead of allowing these things to rule over them.

Godly fathers lay a stable, deeply rooted foundation in the soul of their children that will easily support and foster their accomplishments and endeavors in adulthood. Simply put, the wealth inherited from true fathers becomes a treasure that is passed on from generation to generation among covenant-keeping people.

Our Children Are Inheriting Something
Larger than Themselves

The process of parenting a child includes the crucial task of raising a child's expectations. Our children must understand that they are inheriting something much larger than their parents, themselves or the families they will have someday. They must know that the things Daddy and Mommy are doing today are going to be left for them, and that it is their responsibility to *preserve* the things that they have been taught for their children and their grandchildren. The true wealth of covenant inheritance grows when it is nurtured, cherished and preserved from generation to generation. This is God's way of bringing the stability of His house in heaven into our homes and families on Earth.

True fathers spend time with their children. It is more valuable than any monetary investment in a bank, stockbroker account or land purchase. These things are good and necessary in their proper place. They can all be bought, sold and replaced by anyone equipped with their father's wealth of godly wisdom. Children, however, are the heritage of the Lord.[2] Investments in our children can bear fruit today, tomorrow, next year and 200 years from now! I know that if my father departed from the earth today, then he will have left me (and my siblings) a rich inheritance of godly wealth, of which I have already passed much on to my children.

My father, like any good father, taught me things fully expecting me to embed those same truths in the hearts of my children and of his great-grandchildren. Every father should expect his children to transfer his parental knowledge to their children. This includes his store of wisdom, knowledge, understanding, and above all, the desire to connect with a God larger and greater than he.

One of the most important things we need to do while building covenant with our children is to help them realize that a family is only as good as its name. Once our children realize that they are *in covenant* with their fathers and mothers, they will do anything within their power to protect the integrity for which their parents are known.

I Don't Want Your Gifts—I Want You!

All of this assumes we understand the basic truth that our children need *us*, not the things we buy for them or the gifts with which we surround them. I have seen a father give his children speed boats because he felt guilty for being away from home so long. Yet when this absentee father finally showed up at home, he was surprised to hear his children say, "Daddy, we don't want the things that you give us. All we want is *you*."

These children simply want to want to hear what is in their father's heart. Perhaps they can't quote Jesus' proverb "For where your treasure is, there your heart will be also,"[3] but they know the treasure they long for is locked up in their father's heart. It is the least we can give them as loving parents.

Many parents in industrialized nations tend to give their children what they want instead of what they really need. It is natural for children to ask for what they want, which is rarely what they really need. Fathers and mothers know what their children need, and the first thing every child needs is the love and caring nurture of a father and mother. They have a vital need for the caring protection, support and correction of a father. Again, a good father wants his children to aim higher, go farther and accomplish more than he ever did in his lifetime. But at the very least, every godly parent has the responsibility to make sure their children discover what God wants them to do, and how they are to extend the name of their covenant family. This process requires effective communication between parents and children.

It is a wonderful thing to hear your child tell you how things are going in school, but it is just as important for you to tell them what you are feeling in your heart. This may be especially difficult for you if you are a father, but you need to let your children (and your wife) share in your work and your world.

This heartfelt sharing should be done regularly and with discernment (there are some issues that are best carried to God alone). If your children feel like they are an important part of your world, they won't resent it.

Sow Intimacy to Reap Intimacy with Your Children

The law of sowing and reaping has not been somehow suspended in the area of family communications. We must sow intimacy to reap intimacy. We know that communication is the key to help our children pass through the sometimes difficult years of adolescence, but we rarely want to pay the price to establish trusted lines of communication with our children.

You can count on the fact that your child doesn't know what is in your head unless you share it with them. If you want your child to be transparent, then you have to be transparent too.

Covenant has a way of making life flow. When I go back home to Africa, all of my family members there surround me and we sometimes talk as late as five o'clock in the morning! We talk about everything and express our love for one another in a hundred different ways.

I feel a strong obligation to my children not to isolate them from any credible source of information they need to help them maintain the family tradition. It should be said that there are some aspects of maintaining the family tradition that should not be passed down to the next generation, as well as some that should be. We need to be discerning and pass everything through the grid of a biblical way of thinking and acting. That is the only way my children can continue to reap the benefits of the covenant I enjoy with my father and mother and my siblings in Ghana.

When my daughter, Anna-Kissel, was barely seven years old, I took her with me to visit our homeland in Ghana, Africa. "Anna," I said, "I am going to tell you how Daddy started." When we arrived and the members of my family gathered around us, my child saw her daddy sit among his brothers and sisters and open his heart. She saw me cry (because when you're in covenant, there is no pretense), and she saw me laugh and rejoice with the people of her Ghanaian heritage.

In the area of family communications, we must sow intimacy to reap intimacy.

My children don't see me as an unemotional, macho man. I try to share with them honestly and transparently, whether that means they see me cry or they see me speak with great joy. The result is that my children know that whatever I say to them is coming from the heart. I feel free to cry with them, and they freely cry with me. I've taught them to see me as a human being who has a responsibility to take them beyond my mistakes, beyond my glory and beyond my power.

Teaching God Is Present, Even When I Am Absent

My job is to expose my children to a God who can sustain them *in my absence.* I also have a responsibility to help them gain confidence in their uncles, aunts and cousins who love them very much, each according to their individual giftings and abilities. They are a vital part of God's support network for my family, and I want my children to be intimately acquainted with their strengths, their weaknesses, their accomplishments and their failures. They comprise the covenant family God has given us and they are not to be kept at a distance.

With this in mind, I took my oldest daughter on a family heritage tour throughout Ghana. We stopped in the place where I was born, so I could tell her stories about the foundations of my life and my experiences in Ghana. I would say, "Anna, do you see the chair you are sitting in? Daddy sat in that chair when I was only so many years old, and this is what I did. Do you see that place? That is where I went to nursery, and this is where I did this."

My daughter remembered every story I told her, and it created an attachment and it bonded her heart to her family, her nation and her heritage in Ghana. I knew it was important for her to meet my family and hear them speak the ancient language of our forefathers (even if she cannot speak in that tongue).

If you spend quality time with your children and share the experiences and emotions of your life with them, you will provide them with the things they need to bond to their heritage. It is only when they bond to their covenant heritage that they will begin to take ownership in their family covenant under God and actively work to preserve and expand it.

It is equally important to note that sometimes one's ancestry and what people expect you to pass on to your children and grandchildren may prove to be unbiblical. In such instances, you have to break any covenants that may be associated to evil spirits. Establishing freedom from particular forms of spiritual and emotional oppression is a wonderful legacy to pass on.

Children in Covenant Share Freely with Their Parents

My daughter, Anna-Kissel, is still very young, but she is old enough to like boys and feel those bubbly things in her heart from time to time. With the kind of covenant relationship we share, Anna feels absolutely free to talk with her daddy about any young boy that she likes. She knows that I am vitally concerned about the people she spends time with and the young man she may marry someday. Covenant has been planted in her heart, so she already knows that she is special, and that she just can't afford to elope with someone she meets on a blind date, or show up with someone she met on the plane, to say, "I've found a lover of my heart." Covenant places great value on well-rooted relationships and covenant agreement.

My children have been taught and trained to recognize the earmarks of godly character and integrity in the people around them. It is important for them to discern these things for the protection of their own future, and for the future of my grandchildren. I started praying for grandchildren when Anna was just a young girl. I told her, "I'm praying that as you grow to become the woman God wants you to be, He will send you a man who will help your daddy maintain the name and integrity for which our family tree stands."

Not only do my children know about their family heritage, but they also know their spiritual heritage. They know that their daddy was brought up in a house where we prayed every morning.

We had God's presence in our home, and every day was an adventure in which we experienced peace, unity and love. Beyond that, we were exposed to a God that we felt we couldn't live without. I can still remember how our family used to reminisce and talk about the goodness of God and what He had done when I was little. Not a day went by without us singing the praises of God.

I told my children how I was poisoned in my right eye and hospitalized as a boy. When I came out of the hospital, I was engulfed with conviction over my sin, and I longed for an intimate relationship with the Lord. A passion overtook me that began to change my heart.

I Identified with the Pain of Kids

I felt I just had to scour my neighborhood to see who had eaten and who had not. I felt driven to make sure the hungry received something to eat, even if it meant sharing my own food. When people in need began to seek me, I tried to do what was necessary to feed or clothe them. Somehow I identified with the pains and the problems of the kids in my area and I continued to think often about God during this season. I was acquainted with God, but I sensed there was more. I wanted to personally experience the presence of God in my life.

One Saturday morning I awoke with a gripping conviction and sorrow for humankind. All I can say is that all that day and on Sunday I cried uncontrollably. My parents were concerned because the weeping continued through the day-long church service as I sat with my family; I couldn't even eat.

After we went home, I finally reconciled with God by opening my heart and saying, "God, I know You are with me. I know You are here, but today I am inviting You in. I am making it official. This isn't based on what I learned from Daddy. It isn't based on what I learned from Momma. I want whatever I've learned from them to deepen my personal experience with You, but I want to experience You for myself."

An overwhelming sense of the love and presence of God rolled through me and filled my heart. That evening I did something I had never done before. A supernatural peace came upon me and I fell into a deep sleep. The next morning marked the beginning of a holiday, and I knew everyone in town was home. So I got up and left the room, and the moment my mother saw my face, she said, "Something happened to you!"

Without eating breakfast, washing my face or brushing my teeth that morning, I headed straight for the homes of my friends. When I knocked on the door, my friends' parents would occasionally answer and I would ask, "Is so-and-so here?"

When they said, "Yes, but it's too early," I would reply, "Oh, I'm here to deliver a message." Each time a friend would come to the door, I would tell them one thing: "I've met Him and I'm different." Then I walked away to knock on another door.

Pray That Your Child Has a Rendezvous with Jesus

All my friends heard me share that first brief testimony of divine transformation, then they saw me walk it out day after day. That was the beginning of my journey with the Lord. There were mornings when I would pace up and down the four-mile length of our street with my hands up, praying and worshiping God after our early prayer meetings. I was only 10 or 11 years old, but in Ghana, parents don't think you are crazy if they sense a yearning in your spirit. My parents simply understood that I was having a rendezvous with God, and they respected my hunger for more of Him. It is still considered an honor for God to begin to use a child in a Ghanaian family.

My father and mother were my greatest encouragers, and my father was my foundation. He was the one who personally introduced me to God and taught me about His kingdom. When I began to pray at an early age, I remembered learning about the God of Abraham, Isaac and Jacob. Now at that age, that phrase caused me to remember only two of the generations in the Bible, those of Abraham and Isaac. In my young mind, the third generation is my father, whose Christian name is Jacob (pronounced "Yacob" in Hebrew fashion in Ghana). I saw God in my earthly father (and still do). I saw God work through him and I saw God move upon him powerfully. To this day, when I say "the God of Abraham, Isaac and Jacob," I see the face of my godly father.

When Jesus Christ answered my prayer and the power of God entered my life, I was transformed. The compassion God gave me was so powerful and compelling that I just had to do something. Somehow God empowered me to see what others felt in the sense that I could literally feel their pain as if it were my own.

God Told Me to Help Others Beyond My Own People

The Lord visited me in many vivid ways and touched my life in a manner that compelled me to reach out to the lost and hurting. My evangelical interest was focused on my own people. Later God said to me, "Unless you help others beyond your people, you have not touched your world, because your world is bigger than a little area."

As a teenager, I visited nearby villages on weekends to preach the gospel. On long school holidays (similar to summer vacation in the States), when other students sought kitchen jobs to earn money, I traveled from city to city and village to village to minister the gospel. When I left one town, I would board a bus to the next and preach on the bus en route. I did this for two or more months at a time each holiday, hopping from one bus to another and never really knowing where I was going. I just knew that when the time came, I would take the most direct route back home.

My parents really encouraged me in my teenage itinerant ministry. In the Ghanaian culture, a young man must prove his manhood before he is considered a man, a protector or a provider. For that reason, the most important expression any young man can receive from his father is the statement: "My son, now you are a man." My extended ministry trips by faith to minister in distant towns and villages was my passage to manhood in the spirit, and I think my parents sensed that.

We should thank God for the toughness of our fathers who lovingly push us to do more than they have done, to go where they never went and to learn what they were never privileged to learn. It is because of such determined fathers (and mothers!) that we can be proud of our future.

In every covenantal society, the names of families are covenantal names. A family is known by the reputation it keeps and maintains over the years and generations. Sadly, societal pressures and geographical relocations can fragment family units and diminish the importance of knowing one's family name and its relationship to covenant.

Dishonoring Your Father Brings Shame upon Yourself

In a truly covenantal society, no one wants to go against covenant because it is common knowledge that anyone who destroys or dishonors the name of his father brings shame upon himself and his whole family line. This is spelled out plainly in the Old Testament, and Jesus referred to it while applying it specifically to a religious tradition that went so far that it contradicted the fundamental concepts of Scripture:

> For Moses said, "Honor your father and your mother," and, "Anyone who curses his father or mother must be put to death." But you say that if a man says to his father or mother: "Whatever help you might otherwise have

received from me is Corban" (that is, a gift devoted to God), then you no longer let him do anything for his father or mother. Thus you nullify the word of God by your tradition that you have handed down. And you do many things like that.[4]

Many parents today shower all kinds of things on their children, not seeming to realize that those things are not what their children need. Gifts are wonderful and I love to bless my children with them as much as any other parent. However, I was taught by those wiser than I that there is a difference between *growth* and *maturity*. It is easy to end up with children who are grown but not mature.

Wisdom helps us to mature. Godly parents offer their children more than just gifts because they are after good fruit in their lives. An investment of quality time involves transferring something to our children that can secure them in their future. Time spent cannot be regained; therefore, the best time we can spend with our children is time spent teaching them what we learned with time. So "quality time" is not going to the movies; it is investing our time in the presence of our children and enjoying their company. Then when our children truly *need* something, they should be able to say, "I needed to know this and my father taught me how to do this."

Too Much Influence from Nonparental Sources

Far too many children learn what they know about life from nonparental sources in our surrogate society. Even in the average church setting, if we were to take a poll among the students, we would probably find that many if not most of them were trained about right and wrong more in the classroom than in the home.

Wisdom comes in different ways. It may come through affection, or it may come through discipline, teaching and touching. I often say something that isn't politically correct concerning the ways our fathers give us wisdom, but I say it anyway because it is true. Some of the best wisdom delivered by parents in any culture is the kind that comes unexpectedly from behind at a swift pace. (We tend not to forget the correction and instruction that catches us by surprise.)

The loving and faithful bonds of covenant are the glue that help preserve our homes and anchors our marriages. Covenant covers our weaknesses with unconditional love while applying proper pressure where it does the most good. It sets boundaries and goals for us that bring out the best in our personal character, and covenant provides a safety net when we reach the end of our own resources.

God demonstrated His discipline of covenant when He ordained that each of us be set in a local family and a local Body of Christ—whether we want it or not.[5] We can only reach our potential and fulfill our calling in the heavenly yoke of covenant partnership through the bonds of marriage, family and the Church. Covenant is God's seedbed for greatness in the human heart, the kind of greatness that can span multiple generations and overcome every adversity.

Notes
1. 1 Corinthians 4:15,16.
2. See Psalm 127:3.
3. Matthew 6:21.
4. Mark 7:10-13.
5. See 1 Corinthians 12:18.

churches become
HEALTHIER

CHAPTER 8

The Vital Ingredient

If I had the opportunity to deliver one message to the Church in North America and Europe today, it would be the message of covenant. *All* Christians are bound together in a blood covenant with Jesus Christ and charged to change our world. Yet, our bickering, backbiting and interdenominational rivalries weaken the Church's ability to reach the lost. This is worsened by the false piety we Christians sometimes display; we busy ourselves in church programs and schedules while avoiding and despising the lost. Because *they are not like us*, we do not actively pursue them.

How can we act surprised and offended that non-Christian people don't act, think or live according to Christian principles? On what grounds are we offended? Does God expect nations and governments to reform themselves when it is clearly impossible even for the individual human soul to do this apart from divine intervention? God put the burden for reform and revival squarely on the shoulders of the Church when He said:

> If *my people*, who are *called by my name*, will humble themselves and pray and seek my face and turn from their wicked ways, then will I hear from heaven and will forgive their sin and will heal their land.[1]

Notice that the Lord did not say, "If secular governments—if nations and political leaders who do not call upon My name." According to Jesus Christ, love is supposed to be the one thing that outwardly marks the Church and sets apart the individual people who comprise it. Jesus put it this way:

> A new command I give you: Love one another. As I have loved you, so you *must* love one another. *By this all men will know that you are my disciples, if you love one another.*[2]

Wanted: Christians Who Genuinely Love One Another
Considering the last sentence in this passage from John's Gospel, perhaps we can understand why the world is so confused about what the Church truly is and what it isn't. There may be churches on every corner, but disciples—Christians who love one another according to Christ's unbending criteria—seem to be very hard to find in many areas! This love for one another

transcends cultural differences, liturgical forms, church organization and minor theological distinctions.

The Church needs the message of covenant because the world needs a victorious Church filled with the manifest glory of God. This will never happen until the Church begins to live and walk in the truths of covenant relationship and unconditional love.

In city after city, on television, radio and from our pulpits on every Sunday, Christian voices are raised in loud criticism and condemnation of one another and of our federal and state governments. These harangues are often closed with a hymn or worship song and the prayer, "God, change their lives."

Is it possible that God's reply to those prayers is, "I can't do that while working through hypocrites. You are not in covenant with Me, nor are you in covenant with this nation. You are in covenant with your religion."

As I've said before in these pages, I am convinced that we don't understand covenant. We are living lives that are ruled by convenience and are untouched by covenant. We lack tolerance for those who are different, and we withhold compassion and forgiveness from those who are lost and in sin. Why? It is because there is no covenant in our lives. Without its godly influence and direction, we drift into the deadly waters of hypocrisy, judgmentalism, condemnation and religious guilt-pedaling.

God wants us to retire our pointed fingers of condemnation and pick up our towels of humble servanthood. We have a wonderful example who modeled this for us, even to the point of washing the feet of the man who would betray Him to His enemies and set the stage for His gruesome death.[3]

The Lord wants us to stop assaulting the lost and the broken with attitudes, glances and sometimes literal words that say "What a mess you are! Don't you wish you could be like me, as impossible as that is"; and instead approach them with the compassion of Christ and say, "God loves you and I love you. How can I help?"

For better or for worse, *covenant exposes our true nature.* Covenant only works where there is transparency and honesty. We all need covenant relationships, just as we all need the love and acceptance of others. No one resents people who admire them. No one gets angry because people like them or love them. We want and need all of these things.

God built something into us that longs to give and receive love, acceptance and admiration within the framework of covenant safety and stability. Even God wants to be praised, honored and worshiped, so He took the risks first. He doesn't come to us because He needs something from us, He comes to us because He wants the things we are uniquely equipped to offer Him as creatures made in His own image—praise, worship and freely given love and adoration.

> The dynamic nature of vibrant covenant relationship actually helps me to live up to my potential.

For our part, we don't make covenant with one another because of what we can get out of it. We make covenant because of what we sense God is saying to our hearts, and what we believe we can become and offer to others.

I've learned that when I function in true and strong covenant relationships, not only will I be at my best, but I will be a blessing to others in ways I never dreamed. The dynamic nature of vibrant covenant relationship actually helps me to live up to my potential and achieve the purpose for which I was born. This is why God ordained that we be planted in a local church body; He knows we were created to function best in the environment of covenant relationships.

Covenant Is Vital to Church Government

Covenant, if it is implemented properly, helps remove abuse of power and advantage in local church government. The one who initiates covenant should be the head of the local church, the pastor. Once covenant relationships are established with local leaders, then frankness and openness of communication flourishes. Relationships are healed and restored because people have the freedom to discuss problems, wrongs and abuses.

When church government is only based on the foundation of monetary payment for specified duties, the ministry of the gospel and the oversight of the flock of God is reduced to a mere job performed by a hireling. Since it is not based on covenant, any so-called loyalty to the sheep and the ministry vision is plastic, bank-check loyalty.

Loyalty and dedication is only found in church governments based upon true, biblical covenant relationship. If we're in covenant, we know we are building together. We also know that God called us into the union of spirits supernaturally. In that covenant environment, we are free to value each other's input and experiences. We can really begin to appreciate the blessings and deposits provided by each covenant partner in the local body or leadership group.

Covenant and Leadership Development in the Church

Without covenant, it is impossible to raise up leaders in the Church according to biblical patterns (I call it "God's way").

Seminaries (although not mentioned in God's plan as laid out in the New Testament) do a relatively good job of teaching theological concepts, sound doctrine (according to their particular slant), preaching and counseling techniques, and Church history. However, they generally fail to nurture covenant relationships or teach the transfer or impartation of ethical standards, wisdom and anointing. These things are best taught or caught in the one-on-one intimacy of teacher and disciple.

Before it was time for Elijah to be taken up by the Lord, God led this prophet to a man named Elisha, the son of a prosperous farmer. When Elijah arrived, Elisha was plowing a field with a yoke of oxen while supervising 11 more plowmen with 22 other oxen plowing in front of him at the same time. That is the equivalent of a massive commercial farm operation today.

Elisha had the perfect job situation with every prospect of inheriting the entire farming business from his father. Then Elijah arrived and threw his mantle over Elisha, and everything changed. He left everything behind to follow Elijah, a man he didn't even know. He served him faithfully for 20 years—why?

Most people then and now would say, "What a fool! Not only did this man leave everything to serve an odd stranger who had peculiar ways, but Elisha actually killed his oxen and fed his laborers with them. (This is analogous to a modern farmer selling his tractor and then using the money from the sale to buy dinner for his farmhands.) Elisha made a covenant commitment—the kind you can't go back on. Once he made his choice, Elisha the ex-farmer burned his bridges and left a fortune behind to become a servant with nothing to his name.

It Takes a Follower to Become a Strong Leader
Elisha spent 20 years following in the shadow of Elijah while lis-

tening to the criticism and mocking comments of other would-be prophets who belonged to what the *KJV* calls "the company of the prophets."[4] Although it appears doubtful that any great prophet ever came from these schools, these "Bible students" still felt confident enough to ridicule Elisha the farmer for serving the man of God the way he did. They obviously didn't understand the interrelationship between servanthood and leadership. It takes a follower to become a strong leader—followers are the only people God trusts with His greatest gifts.

When Elijah announced that God was sending him to Bethel, he told Elisha not to come, but Elisha refused to leave his master. As soon as they reached Bethel, the "Bible students" from the Bethel School of the Prophets came out all together to taunt their favorite bald-headed victim: "The company of the prophets at Bethel came out to Elisha and asked, 'Do you know that the LORD is going to take your master from you today?' 'Yes, I know,' Elisha replied, 'but do not speak of it.'"[5]

As far as we know, Elisha's hecklers were probably still laughing in the background when Elijah the prophet again announced a change in plans. He told Elisha that God was sending him to Jericho, and again told his assistant to stay put. Elisha refused to leave his master once again, so off they went to Jericho.

The same scenario unfolds as all of the sneering Bible students at the Jericho School of the Prophets turned up to stare at Elisha and offer their nuggets of wisdom: "The company of the prophets at Jericho went up to Elisha and asked him, 'Do you know that the LORD is going to take your master from you today?' 'Yes, I know,' he replied, 'but do not speak of it.'"[6]

Finally, Elijah announced that God was sending him to the Jordan River, and once again Elisha refused to leave his master. Fifty students from the school of the prophets followed the pair to the remote area near the Jordan and watched from a safe distance to see what would happen. Elijah divided the waters of the Jordan with his cloak and the two men crossed over. There the prophet finally asked Elisha what he could do for him before the Lord took him. Elisha had thought about this for 20 years, and he said without hesitation, "Let me inherit a double portion of your spirit."[7] Only disciples who are in covenant relationship with their instructors in the Lord can ask such a thing.

Elisha's Hecklers Suddenly Had a Change of Heart

Elisha's request was granted and he was able to work twice as many miracles as Elijah during his ministry. It is interesting to notice that the Bible students who had been Elisha's hecklers suddenly had a change of heart when they saw Elisha part the same river Elijah had parted in front of their eyes. The Bible says, "The company of the prophets from Jericho, who were watching, said, 'The spirit of Elijah is resting on Elisha.' And they went to meet him and bowed to the ground before him."[8] It all began when a man of God interrupted Elisha's life with the call of God and the chance to be discipled in the school of covenant relationship and servanthood.

Joshua wasn't looking for a job either when Moses permanently interrupted his life with a covenant relationship that would go beyond Moses' lifetime. According to the book of Numbers, Joshua served as Moses' aide from his youth. In fact, Moses had even changed his name from "Deliverer" (Hoshea) to "The Lord is Salvation" (Joshua).[9]

The first time we hear of Joshua in the book of Exodus, Moses suddenly calls him and tells him to pick out some men and fight the Amalekites. While Aaron and Hur stayed up on a hill and helped hold up Moses' hands, it was Joshua who risked his life at Moses' word, in faith that the "staff of God" would release God's favor and bring victory.[10]

It is significant that after Joshua and his men obeyed the word of the Lord through Moses, God singled out Joshua and said:

Then the LORD said to Moses, "Write this on a scroll as something to be remembered *and make sure that Joshua hears it*, because I will completely blot out the memory of Amalek from under heaven." Moses built an altar and called it The LORD is my Banner. He said, "For hands were lifted up to the throne of the LORD. The LORD will be at war against the Amalekites from generation to generation."[11]

Servanthood and faithfulness to covenant relationships in God's kingdom positions us for greatness and blessings from on high. Joshua's key role in the battle set him up to be one of two selected witnesses on the day the Lord revealed yet another of His holy names—Jehovah Nissi, God my Banner.[12]

Joshua went everywhere Moses went. If Moses went to the tent of meeting to meet God, Joshua went with him (with or without an invitation—it is often one of the privileges of true covenant relationship). Later in their relationship, when Moses stepped down from Mount Sinai to talk to the people about what God had said, Joshua stayed behind alone, soaking in the presence of God that he had come to love.[13] He found the place called "there," and he learned how to be at the right place at the right time through covenant faithfulness.

The things Joshua saw in the secret places of God equipped and prepared him to speak as a man of valor in the face of seemingly impossible odds. When the time came for the leadership of the Israelites to change hands, God spoke to Moses about His choice of a leader:

So the LORD said to Moses, "Take Joshua son of Nun, *a man in whom is the spirit, and lay your hand on him.* Have him stand before Eleazar the priest and the entire assembly and commission him in their presence. *Give him some of your authority* so the whole Israelite community will obey him. He is to stand before Eleazar the priest, who will obtain decisions for him by inquiring of the Urim before the LORD. At his command he and the entire community of the Israelites will go out, and at his command they will come in."[14]

This passage shows us how the anointing or mantle of God could be transferred from one person to another in the Old Testament. The Hebrew word translated as "authority" in the *NIV* and as "honor" in the *KJV* is *howd* (hode). It means "grandeur," or an "imposing form and appearance: beauty, comeliness, excellency, glorious, glory, honor, majesty."[15] These are the things Moses received while in the presence of God as a part of his divine mantle of leadership.

Joshua already had the distinction of "having the spirit" in him by lingering in the presence of God. Here he also received an impartation of Moses' leadership anointing and it sealed his commission as God's warrior-leader who would possess the Promised Land. (The process of impartation through the laying on of hands is even more straightforward and prominent in the New Testament Church.[16])

Leadership Anointing Comes Through Servanthood

Prayer is godly and necessary in every area of the Christian life, but you don't get a leadership anointing solely by prayer—you get it through servanthood. You need to read the Word of God daily, but you don't get a leadership anointing by reading the Word—you get it through servanthood. Servanthood may take the form of a determination and desire to follow and assist your pastor if God's anointing is upon him. In general, it is marked by a commitment to stick close to the anointing.

This goes contrary to our flesh because we live in an independent society where we like to say, "We don't follow anybody—we hear God for ourselves." It is true that God speaks to each of His children, but it is also true that He chooses to work through flawed human leaders, whether we like it or not. He has chosen to follow a process in which He separates people for a purpose and prepares them for leadership through a season of servanthood until they are ready. The greatest leaders are servants. Anytime we try to shorten or avoid this process, we become a hindrance to the glory of God.

Both the anointing and iniquity can be rubbed off on you by association. Carefully choose the people with whom you spend your time. If you hang around the wrong folks, they will take you to the wrong places. If you hang around those who are led by the Spirit, they will take you into the presence and purpose of God. God-hungry people say, "Lord, I am going to stick with this thing. I won't back off until I get what I need." This kind of persistence shows up when the people of God pursue Him corporately as well.

God Said It Is Time for You to Come

A group of ministers in India were seeking God when He gave them a vision in which they saw me preaching to large crowds in their nation. They had never met me before, but they obeyed the vision and sent me a fax that arrived in the middle of the night. I heard the fax machine and I got up and read it immediately. It said, "We want you to come to India. God said it is time for you to come here, and it is very important." (I had already told my church that God had laid a burden on my heart to go to India.)

I contacted this group and said, "I want to come to India, but I want to make sure that you organize this thing quite well. I am expecting to minister to at least 50,000 people in the meetings." They said, "No problem. Our church just held a picnic at the beach and 100,000 people showed up. We have 7,000 home-group leaders and 128 district pastors working under five senior pastors. We are touching India for God, and we want you to come. We are expecting 1 million people because they are hungry. God told us if you come here, He will be creating miracles that have never been done in this part of the world."

When they said, "God told us," I had to make sure. "God told you?" I asked. They said, "Yes, God told us. We are sure." I didn't tell them what God told me until after I had tested the waters. I could commit myself to come because I was finally assured that these men had been to the mountain of God. They pressed in to the heart of God until they found themselves in the place called "there." They heard things that they would not have heard if they had stayed home and done nothing to reach their nation for Christ. This is the way covenant people get things done in the kingdom of God. Covenant is not apathetic; it is aggressive, persistent and expectant in the unity of Christ.

We need covenant in the Body of Christ. If we are in covenant, then whatever we ask God in unity, we will receive. On the other hand, whenever we *break* covenant, we can be sure that God will not answer our prayers. We see this in Peter's instruction to husbands:

Husbands, in the same way *be considerate as you live with your wives*, and treat them with *respect* as the weaker partner and *as heirs with you* of the gracious gift of life, so that nothing will *hinder your prayers*.[17]

Why Do the Prayers of Many Christian Men "Bounce off the Ceiling"?

God didn't say a wife's prayers would be hindered, because He knows the creature wearing the pants is the one who has the big problem with ego and pride. Men tend to pray only when they are in trouble. Here is the difficult part: If "living with our wives according to knowledge" is God's criteria for answered prayer, then the prayers of perhaps 95 percent of all the men who call themselves Christians are "bouncing off the ceiling." Why? Because *they don't know how to live in covenant*.

When there is confusion in my home, I don't bother to pray any kind of prayer except the prayer of repentance. Anything else is a waste of time and breath. When I have anything against my wife or when we are in disagreement, I don't pray unless I begin first with a prayer of repentance. Why? Because I know God is not going to answer my prayers when I am in sin. When I repent, He always says, "Go fix it. Give up your pride and fix it, macho man. Don't be silly." If I offer any kind of answer other than "Yes Lord," I hear only silence in heaven.

Once we fix our sin problems and come into unity, powerful things begin to happen. If one person can rout a thousand enemies, according to the Bible,[18] then imagine what happens when the whole house is in agreement! What can happen if an entire local church body comes into agreement in the name of Jesus? What could be accomplished in that city and region by a church that saw every prayer it made answered in power for all to see?

Now we can understand why the adversary works so hard to prevent the Church from coming into unity. He wants us to ignore the little foxes that spoil the vine[19] until those small irritations bring about great disunity.

David's Favorite Son Became His Worst Enemy

We singled out King David as a noteworthy covenant keeper in a previous chapter, and we also noted that he was human and therefore imperfect. One of his errors as a father involved the favoritism he showed to a son named Absalom, born of his Canaanite wife, Maacah.

In time, Absalom revealed his true nature with the carefully planned cold-blooded murder of his brother Amnon in retaliation for his vicious rape of their sister, Tamar. Absalom fled in exile to Syria and was finally invited back by his father. After spending two years in Jerusalem, forbidden to see his father's face, Absalom finally schemed his way back into David's presence and was restored to his father's good graces. He immediately launched a scheme to steal his father's throne.

In only four years, Absalom used his God-given gifts to engineer a successful coup, and he even managed to steal away the loyalty of one of David's most trusted counselors. He did it in the same way people split churches today—through smooth flattery, secret assurances of understanding and empathy with the concerns of the people (as opposed to what they are likely to receive from those in authority), and by making people believe he was one of them—one of the lowly people outside of the decision-making process.

As the word went out, "Absalom is king in Hebron," David ordered the evacuation of his palace in Jerusalem and urged his staff to leave him and save themselves. Only the day before, Ittai the Gittite had left his home town of Gath in Philistia along with 600 men to accompany King David back to Jerusalem.

Their conversation illustrates the life-changing power of covenant:

> The king said to Ittai the Gittite, "Why should you come along with us? Go back and stay with King Absalom. *You are a foreigner, an exile from your homeland. You came only yesterday. And today shall I make you wander about with us, when I do not know where I am going?* Go back, and take your countrymen. May kindness and faithfulness be with you." But Ittai replied to the king, "As surely as the LORD lives, and as my lord the king lives, wherever my lord the king may be, *whether it means life or death, there will your servant be.*" David said to Ittai, "Go ahead, march on." So Ittai the Gittite marched on with all his men and the families that were with him.[20]

This is true covenant in action. It goes beyond mere words to concrete action in the face of risk, uncertainty, and the possible loss of reputation.

Covenant Relationship Is the Surest Cure for Absalom

The spirit of Absalom is still alive and well in our churches. When it isn't dealt with, it can bring devastating division to a local church body. The surest cure for an active spirit of Absalom in a local church is the same cure God used in David's life: He gave him covenant partners who stood by him in faith and refused to run. God always redeems the righteous and brings down the conspirator in the end.[21]

True covenant relationships in the Church contain no hint of compulsion or pressure. Once those things enter the picture, we are creating unison action by force, not covenant unity in love.

God wants to establish His covenant with the Church. He longs for a body of believers with whom He can walk in sweet communion. He has already given His life for us. Now it is our turn.

If you are in covenant, you won't get an "attitude" every time someone in the church disagrees with you or does something that irritates you. As a covenant keeper, you should know that covenant demands personal responsibility and intimate honesty. Your relationships must be built on truth, no matter how unlovely it may be. Once you extend covenant to someone else and it is received, you don't break that covenant. (If you make a vow and you break it prematurely, you bring curses upon yourself. It is best for you not to make the vow than to break the vow.)[22]

Enter into covenant with fellow believers knowing you are all human and are prone to failure and mistakes from time to time. Stand with each other in your embarrassing and miserable failures as well as in your shining moments of success. That is covenant, not friendship for the sake of convenience. It includes the freedom to correct or rebuke one another in love when necessary. Although you may grow angry with each other, you are committed to keep loving each other and working it out. Covenant frees you to be yourself. Jesus demonstrated this kind of transparency in His covenant relationship with His disciples.

Covenant even causes us to share reputations, an act that transcends convenience or politically correct positions. Paul shared his reputation with a runaway slave named Onesimus. The book of Philemon is simply Paul's letter to the Christian owner of Onesimus:

> I appeal to you for my son Onesimus, who became my
> son while I was in chains. . . . He is very dear to me but
> even dearer to you, both as a man and as a brother in the

Lord. So *if you consider me a partner*, welcome him as you would welcome me. *If he has done you any wrong or owes you anything, charge it to me.* I, Paul, am writing this with my own hand. *I will pay it back.*[23]

This is true covenant on display: The apostle was telling Philemon that if Onesimus had any debts or obligations, he would absorb the costs.

Some people will die to protect their covenant relationships. Some people will take time off work to care for their friends when they get sick. When a friend calls to say he is stranded on the road at three o'clock in the morning, he can count on their help—they are in covenant. This kind of relationship is all too rare in the Body of Christ today, and God is out to change that.

God has blessed me with some wonderful covenant brothers who work with me in the ministry. Covenant plays a large role in my ministry, so we take it very seriously. We made a covenant together by heart and by relationship. When I sensed that the Lord wanted me to give special covenant rings to those with whom I am in covenant, I acted on that leading. The first man I talked to about it had become like a son to me. When I told him the Lord laid it on my heart to enter into a covenant with him, he sat there and wept. I gave him the ring and told him its purpose was merely to remind him of the covenant. He said, "Why do you want to make covenant with me? I have nothing to offer you."

"That's why I'm making covenant with you," I said. "The one who initiates covenant always has more to lose than the one who responds to covenant." That is the way it has always been. When God made covenant with Abraham, He had much more to lose than Abraham, the moon worshiper. Jesus made covenant with us, and we know we had nothing to offer Him. God gave us His only Son to restore covenant with us. When you make covenant with someone in the Body of Christ, it is like saying, "I am willing to give my life for you." Jesus put it this way:

> Greater love has no one than this, that he lay down his life for his friends. You are my friends if you do what I command. I no longer call you servants, because a servant does not know his master's business. Instead, I have called you friends, for everything that I learned from my Father I have made known to you. You did not choose me, but I chose you and appointed you to go and bear fruit—fruit that will last. Then the Father will give you whatever you ask in my name. This is my command: Love each other.[24]

This is the essence of covenant. If we are in covenant with God, then we are willing to give our lives for His cause and for our brothers and sisters in Christ.

Notes
1.   2 Chronicles 7:14, italics mine.
2.   John 13:34,35, italics mine.
3.   See John 13:2-15.
4.   1 Samuel 10:5,10; 19:20; 2 Kings 2:3,5,7,15; 4:1,38; 5:22; 6:1; 9:1.
5.   2 Kings 2:3.
6.   2 Kings 2:5.
7.   2 Kings 2:9.
8.   2 Kings 2:15.
9.   See Numbers 11:28 and 13:16, respectively.
10. Exodus 17:9-13.
11. Exodus 17:14-16, italics mine.
12. See Exodus 17:15.
13. See Exodus 33:11.
14. Numbers 27:18-21, italics mine.
15. James Strong, *Strong's Exhaustive Concordance of the Bible* (Peabody, MA: Hendrickson Publishers, n.d.), meanings and definitions drawn from the word derivations for "honor" *(KJV)* or "authority" *(NIV)* (Hebrew, #1935).

16. See Acts 8:18; 1 Timothy 4:14; Hebrews 6:2.

17. 1 Peter 3:7, italics mine.

18. See Joshua 23:10.

19. See Song of Solomon 2:15.

20. 2 Samuel 15:19-22, italics mine.

21. See Psalm 7:9; 37:38; 73:17; Matthew 13:19; 2 Thessalonians 1:5.

22. See Numbers 30:2.

23. Philemon 10,16-19, italics mine.

24. John 15:13-17, italics mine.

broken lives are
RESTORED

CHAPTER 9

How to Rebuild God's Way

How do we bring biblical covenant principles into the lives of people who have no history of covenant relationship or faithfulness in their life experience? How do we introduce covenant to wounded children from dysfunctional homes or to married couples who did everything wrong before they met Christ and are now "reaping the whirlwind" in their relationships?[1]

All of us come to Christ as sinners, but more and more of us are coming to Him after our sins and decades of running have scarred and broken us on the inside. God saves and transforms our spirits instantly, but after years spent in a lifestyle that is not based on God, we come with a heavy load of baggage attached to our souls (the mind, will and emotions).

Even though we are saved by the power of God, we have to retrain our thought patterns and physical appetites to line up with God's Word and standards of conduct. The apostle Paul said, "He [the believer, the member of the Body of Christ] who *has been stealing* must steal no longer, but must work, *doing something useful with his own hands*, that he may have something to share with those in need."[2]

This is the daily nitty-gritty side of covenant relationship in the Body of Christ. How do we bring covenant to people who have never even been exposed to covenant? We need to answer this question because American life in the new millennium is clearly different than it was even during the last half century.

The epidemic of divorce (both in the general population and in the Church) has rapidly speeded the breakdown of the family unit in society. Now we are seeing evidence of second-generation dysfunctional and fractured families producing even more "children of divorce."

When someone comes into God's kingdom as the product of two or three generations of family dysfunction, the Church is faced with a difficult rebuilding project. It is roughly equivalent to third-generation slaves in post-Civil War America in the late 1800s trying to reclaim the tribal history and social stability their great-grandfathers and great-grandmothers once had.

God instituted covenant as a way to put heavenly stability into earthly instability. The principles of covenant relationship and covenant living in Christ are a sure lifeline for new Christians hampered by life's scars and past betrayals and failures. As long as we have covenant, we can handle anything. Whether we find ourselves trapped in the ravages of war, pestilence, imminent death or terminal disease, we will find that covenant relationships and covenant living are God's way of bringing heaven to earth.

We Have Celebrated Worldly Wisdom
Rather than Godly Wisdom

The covenant restoration process begins with knowledge, wisdom and honesty, but we have celebrated our intelligence instead of recognizing godly wisdom and divine principle. Covenant is a principle, a heavenly stronghold that can only be entered through the door of truth. The first step toward restoration is the open admission of wrongdoing. When we attempt to do what is right apart from the power of God, we are building with the unstable components of wood, hay and stubble. When fiery tests come (and they will), all we have left are ashes blowing in the wind.

Society makes it difficult for us to admit we need help, especially when divine help comes only after we recognize and admit that our elaborate efforts to be good aren't good enough.

Secondly, restoration only comes when we are willing to embrace change. Change insults arrogance and pride, and it has a way of reducing stubbornness. Thirdly, we must be willing to let down the guards of pride. If pride has its way in your life, you will begin to believe that you are indispensable and no one has the right to correct or instruct you.

We have forgotten that there are some ancient landmarks we cannot remove. If you decide to build a house, remember that the most important part of the house is not the structure. First make sure you spend enough time, effort and money to lay a proper foundation; then concern yourself with how the house is going to look. As Jesus taught His disciples, if you don't have a proper foundation, you will suffer a complete collapse when the wind, the storm and the rain come to test it.

Once we admit we have failed and need help, embrace change, and lower our guards of pride, the Holy Spirit will take hold of our lives and lead us into God's perfect will. The Holy Spirit's job is to take us into areas we have never been before—if we allow Him to take us there.

Covenant and the Restoration of the Home

Any pastor, family counselor or social worker who is in agreement with the biblical principles of covenant can tell you that most dysfunctional or broken homes are not built on covenant. Most couples seem to build their relationship and homes on "likeness," or shared ideas about what they want in life. Unfortunately, what we want is not necessarily what we need. Perhaps this helps explain why so many couples spend a fortune to have an elaborate wedding, hoping in the back of their minds that they will not spend the rest of their married lives in divorce court fighting over what is left after their "house of wants" falls apart.

> The truth is never based on what we want; it is always based on what we need.

In a home based on covenant, it is common for young people contemplating marriage to hear their mother or father say to them privately, "Son, you have to be careful of this woman; she's not the kind of woman for you. Son, you've got to be careful. Daughter, you have to be careful. You know this man's background; he didn't come from a covenantal home, so make sure you are extra cautious."

We are all well aware of the damage that can be caused by controlling parents who try to dictate every aspect of their children's lives, but this is not what I am talking about. Covenant *requires us to be involved* in the lives of our loved ones. God's Word, our supreme guide for covenant living, puts it this way:

> *Speaking the truth in love*, we will in all things grow up into him who is the Head, that is, Christ. From him the whole body, joined and held together by every supporting ligament, grows and builds itself up in love, *as each part does its work.*[3]

Covenant requires loving parents to tell their children what very few, if any, friends will tell them: the uncomfortable *truth*. The truth is never based on what we want; it is always based on what we *need*, or what God in His wisdom requires.

Many Family Decisions Are Wrongly Dictated by the "God of the Job"

We have allowed our jobs to take first place in our lives, and our jobs—rather than God—determine where we live. We all have to feed, clothe and house our families, but if God is God (and He is), then He is well able to supply us with a job in the city or region where He has "planted" us. It is simply a matter of faith-activated obedience. When we allow our jobs to dictate such crucial family decisions as where we live, fellowship and raise our children, we are allowing our decisions to be wrongly dictated by the "god of the job."

When jobs dictate our lives, families find themselves scattered geographically, and in many cases we can't reclaim the virtues and benefits of the nuclear or extended family. God seems to understand this problem because the New Testament seems to offer us some guidelines for recreating a spiritual nuclear family. Many of the Grecian congregations in Asia Minor had immigrated from Greece and were experiencing some of the same problems we face today with our mobile society.

Geographic separation has robbed us of the sound advice of parents, grandparents, and aunts and uncles; but the apostle Paul urged his disciple, Titus, to "teach the older women to be reverent in the way they live . . . to teach what is good. Then they can train the younger women to love their husbands and children."[4] He also wrote, "Similarly, encourage the young men to be self-controlled. In everything set them an example by doing what is good."[5] This is God's way of providing a surrogate family for us through covenant.

One thing I've noticed is that women in general seem to understand and honor covenant more than men. Perhaps this is because they instinctively understand the value of emotions, passion and compassion. I have to tell you that if you don't have a heart that shows emotions, then you cannot be in covenant.

Covenant Is Sealed and Upheld with Passion

On the face of it, a covenant is an objective, factual commitment or legal agreement that is sealed and upheld with passion. It takes all three parts of our being to keep covenant—body, soul and spirit. Just as logic alone cannot propel a man to heroism for the sake of his Savior or his country, only passion and conviction from the core of a person's being can produce the selfless service of covenant. We won't lay down our lives for a real estate or business contract—we lay them down for Him who died for us, and for our families, our brothers and sisters in Christ, and for the lost. Covenant is perceived, received and lived from the heart, not the head.

The God of covenant looks at our hearts. When He discovers a pure heart, there is nothing He will hold back. Have you ever prayed, "Lord, today is the day I am broken for You"? Our usual pattern is to walk out of His presence and promptly go to work trying to fix ourselves. We leave His presence feeling flushed and empowered, and we begin to think that we can put ourselves back together again. The problem is that unless we allow God to fix us, He will have to keep breaking us until we let Him fix us. Christians who live in a perpetual state of brokenness are sometimes unwilling to be mended by God.

God is taking the Church through a process of brokenness so that He can remake Her and restore her to her spotless destiny. This isn't the time to question what God is doing; it is time for us to keep going without looking back at our individual "Gomorrahs." God wants to establish the true covenant of heaven in our lives, our homes and in our churches, but there are some things that have to drop off and be left behind forever. Don't let your heart be troubled lest you get dismayed. Trust Him to lead you through to wholeness.

When God sees that you are determined to seek Him, He will do what needs to be done to meet you where you are. There is a place in God called "there"; and if you are curious enough, bold enough and determined enough to go after Him, you will end up in the secret place of His presence. Once you reach that place, God will call you even further and deeper into Himself. When that happens, don't give in to the temptation to step back and congratulate yourself or launch a ministry based on your experiences. God can make any place His living room, and it is usually in places most people will never find.

God Leads Us to Places We Have Never Been

The Bible says that whoever is a son or daughter of God is led by the Spirit of God.[6] Regardless of your history or spiritual pedigree, being led by God means He will lead you to places you have never been. He will not take you to places you have been, because those places and situations comprise your experience, not your place of faith.

Be careful when you tell the Lord, "Where You lead me, I will follow." He takes you at your word and expects you to keep it as a covenant promise. Never expect God to take you through short-cuts. He is more likely to take you through the back side of the desert for a season of training. Once you ask Him to lead you, then have the decency and fortitude to follow Him faithfully.

Spiritually phony Christians often say, "God told me this . . ." If they are right, then everything God is saying seems to be a lie because we never see any action on earth backing up those communications from heaven. When God really tells you to do something, you don't talk much about it—you *do* it. Too many of us have a "brownie-point mentality" in the Church. We only do things for the sake of the recognition of man. Our reward for true assignments from God does not come from man, it comes from Him.

No matter how low we have sunk in the depths of sin or where we come from, God always calls us higher. And when God calls us to a place we have never been, He will provide for us. When Jesus told Peter to let down his nets, he obeyed despite his previous failure and fatigue. His obedience yielded a net-breaking harvest of fish that took the strength of two boat crews to bring to shore. So it is with God's direction to His covenant children. Expect God to lead you to unexpected places, and don't be surprised if there are thorns and storms along the way. He wants to teach you how to go through thorny situations and stormy seasons without failing or faltering.

Who Told You the Boot Camp of Covenant Was Fun?

When we experience opposition or difficulty, many of us are

tempted to say, "Well, if there was a God, this would not have happened." Perhaps we entered the situation in our own strength and God is allowing us to tackle it our way until our way is shaken loose. When God leads us, He trains our hands to war. How many people who served in the armed services have told you that boot camp was fun? Who told you the boot camp of covenant was fun? God allows us to sweat and strain, and teaches us to "gut it out" through our trials so we won't quit when we are under fire. We need to learn to trust Him when He says He will never leave us.

The ultimate secret of restoration in the Church is God Himself. He ultimately works through the framework of covenant relationships, but the Source of all healing, restoration, renewal and miracles is God. He brings deliverance in ways beyond our experience or comprehension. He is amazing! He unsettles the things and abilities we like to call "normal" and supernaturally transforms and uses the things we dismiss as "abnormal" or unworthy of notice. When God takes hold of your life, He never goes the way you planned to go. You will never be the same when you encounter His presence.

At times you may look at yourself and say, "I can't believe this is me. I was the filthiest person in the city. My language was filthy, my mind was polluted, and my life was wicked beyond words. But then God changed me." My friend, the God of covenant, the God of the Cross and the empty tomb makes everything beautiful in its time. The God of covenant is the God of miraculous restoration, and He reaches out to us when we have nothing to offer Him but our hearts. This is the mystery of restoration in God's family of covenant.

Jesus Rarely Spent Time with Synagogue People
The synagogues and the Temple in Jesus' day had become walls,

or fortresses of tradition. They were so religious that only the pious were welcome there. Even Jesus Christ found it difficult to deal with them because they felt they "had it all." The same is true today. It is very easy to miss the essence of God's worship for the sake of observing the lifeless traditions of man. Not all traditions are bad,[7] but not everything in the Church is of God. Men can and have killed others in the name of the Lord. Tradition can be a serial killer that still roams our church aisles today. Jesus said, "You nullify the word of God for the sake of your tradition."[8]

Jesus Christ did not find His disciples in the Temple. They actually lived outside the Temple in the marketplace, and sometimes lived on the very fringes of society. They were on the highways and the byways. In other words, they were "street people." To be honest, God does not seek to restore the religious;[9] He seeks those who recognize their desperate need, whether they are in the Church or not. Sheep safely resting in the "fold," are not God's top priority.[10] Yes, He loves believers, but we need to remember that He came to save that which was lost.[11] So God's primary burden is for those far away from Him, including those who don't frequent our church services.

Jesus warned the disciples toward the end of His earthly ministry that He was going to leave them. He also warned them, "I want you to know that when I leave you, the very people who kicked you out of the Temple will try to kill you as they did Me. They will think they are doing God a service because you don't fit in their traditional ways of worship or celebration."[12]

Jesus demonstrated the "here is the truth even though you don't want to hear it" aspect of covenant relationship when He said, "Because I have said these things, *you are filled with grief. But I tell you the truth*: It is for your own good that I am going away."[13]

Painful Truth Is Better than a Comfortable Lie

The Bible says that when we discover and know Him who is Truth, the truth will set us free.[14] The truth may hurt, but those in covenant must always prefer the painful truth to the comfortable lie. Truth is the door to restoration for the hurting, the wounded and the broken who come into God's house of covenant. The Spirit of Truth, God the Holy Spirit, is the most prominent agent of restoration in our lives. Jesus said: "But when he, the Spirit of truth, comes, he will guide you into all truth."[15]

Jesus knows about our past, yet He is ready to walk with us into our future. That is the way you and I are to approach all of our covenant relationships. True covenant friends don't offer or withdraw their support and love depending on the mood they are in. Covenant isn't built upon "passing relationships."

The hypocritical religion of the Pharisees would never reach out to the prostitutes, paupers, sinners and lepers as Jesus did. Neither will our wants-based version of Christianity. Jesus is still reaching out to the broken, the downcast and the discarded people of the world. Did we get left behind somehow? The only way we can reach out to broken people and establish true, lifelong covenant relationships with them is through transparent, unconditional, covenant love.

One of the funniest things I've seen in the Body of Christ is the way we try our very best to avoid making a mistake in front of our fellow believers! Why? We know the local "Pharisee committee" is just waiting to help crucify us to rid the church of such a religious blemish. Do you have the feeling that if you get "wounded in the war of life" in your church, then some of your brethren may line up to help finish you off?

The end result of all of this religious pretense is that everyone who belongs to the church social club feels compelled to live a perpetual lie. They fear that if they ever let people know who and what they really are, their religious life will be over. If the preacher says, "Come to the altar if you have bitterness in your heart. Come and get it fixed," the more honest members of the congregation are telling themselves, *God better kill me in my seat. I am not going to the altar, because if I show up down there, the next day the whole church will say I have bitterness in my heart.* Unfortunately, they are probably right!

When the spirit of covenant is missing from a local body of Christ, it forces its members to pretend that everything is going well even when they feel like they are dying. We don't need to go to Hollywood or take acting classes if the people sitting beside us are forcing us to master the art of pretense in the name of survival and religious perfection. If you cannot come to church and be yourself, then my friend, you are not living in true covenant.

They Fell Due to the Importance of Pretense

The fear of man can kill or wound the strongest among us. I have known people who held some of the most powerful places of position in the business world. When they lost their jobs, they couldn't bear to tell their friends and family that they had lost their jobs. Due to the importance of pretense in their lives, they felt they had to play the game and eventually started writing bad checks. By the time the truth came out, it was too late. People would have helped them, but because they operated in purely surface relationships, they kept up the pretense at any cost until their actions put them in prison.

Covenant relationship is founded upon unconditional love and commitment. People in covenant do not keep a record of wrongs or remember yesterday's pain. They act to support, correct, restore and preserve.

Covenant causes us to do things we can never explain. When people in covenant with you are in trouble, you just reach out in spite of the cost or the obstacles. I have known parents who died in fires because they did not want to escape without their babies. I have seen people killed because they saw a big truck moving at full speed toward a little child in the middle of the road. They could not stand to see the little child crushed, and they instinctively rushed into the path of the truck to save that child! Many times, caring people will even die with the very person they are trying to save.

Covenant Love Goes Beyond Words to Heartfelt Action

Covenant relationship is not spooky and religious. It is simply the kind of love that goes beyond words to heartfelt action. It isn't rooted in our abilities or personal virtues; it is enabled and directed by the power of God within us. He expects us to love others—including the unlovely among us—as He has loved us. That means we are to love in deed rather than in word only. Covenant love does not come through the intellect, it comes by the Spirit of God.

Even our covenant with Him is empowered by the Holy Spirit in our hearts. He is at work when we find ourselves in a terrible situation and praying from the heart, "Lord, no matter what happens, I will still forever be grateful. If I never sing again, if I never preach or hold a job again, Lord, I will not let it make me bitter. I will remain thankful and I will still serve You with a thankful heart."

We are talking about covenant. He wants the love that we have for Him to be shown to one another. He says to not say we love a God that we don't see when we don't love the brother that we see. The love that we show to a brother is a reflection of the love we have for God. If we have God's kind of love, then that love becomes a covenant love. God knows nothing but covenant love. He is looking for a Church where the believers are in covenant with each other, who will rejoice with those who rejoice and weep with those who weep.[16] That kind of unconditional love only comes when we are in covenant through Christ. If you say you love, you have to quantify your claim. Don't just say, "I love you, brother." The proof of your words is in your deeds. You have to go beyond mere words to see the broken remade, and the lost restored.

Notes
1. See Hosea 8:7.
2. Ephesians 4:28, italics mine.
3. Ephesians 4:15,16, italics mine.
4. Titus 2:3,4.
5. Titus 2:6,7.
6. See Romans 8:14.
7. See 1 Corinthians 11:2; 2 Thessalonians 2:15.
8. Matthew 15:6.
9. See Mark 2:15.
10. See Matthew 18:12-14. The Good Shepherd loves and cherishes all of the "ninety-nine sheep" in His fold, but He will go the extra mile to recover and restore the sheep who are lost. He wants us to have the same desire to seek and save the lost, the discarded and the disregarded.
11. See Matthew 18:11, *KJV.*
12. This is my paraphrased version of John 16:2.
13. John 16:6,7, italics mine.
14. See John 8:31,36.
15. John 16:13.
16. See Romans 12:15.

BLESSINGS
too numerous to count

CHAPTER 10

Obedience Counts

The benefits of covenant are almost too numerous to mention, yet many Christians today don't even know that covenant exists. People flock to seminars by the hundreds of thousands to learn how to receive the blessings of God. They want to know how to be prosperous and succeed in today's competitive world.

I don't blame people for wanting to know these things, but as Christians, we should understand that God's blessings encompass far more than the acquisition or accumulation of money. Yes, He wants to bless us with success and prosperity in every way because we are His children. However, His blessings come because we honor His covenant and keep His Word, not simply because we ask for success and prosperity.

Children quickly learn that gifts and blessings flow from their parents. However, they also learn that although their parents' love is unconditional, certain blessings come *only in response to obedience*, no matter how much they ask or beg for them. In the same way, there is place for prayers of request and petitions, but the Lord's covenant blessings are reserved for covenant keepers, or "doers of the Word."[1]

John the apostle was a covenant keeper with a track record for training the people of God to love and nurture one another. He wrote:

> The elder, to my dear friend Gaius, whom I love in the truth. Dear friend, I pray *that you may enjoy good health* and that *all may go well with you* [that you may "*prosper*," *KJV*], even as your soul is getting along well. It gave me great joy to have some brothers come and tell about your faithfulness to the truth and how you continue to walk in the truth. *I have no greater joy than to hear that my children are walking in the truth.* Dear friend, *you are faithful in what you are doing for the brothers, even though they are strangers to you.* They have told the church about your love.[2]

John was a "new covenant man," and in this passage he is praising a member of his covenant family for honoring and practicing the principles of covenant. Gaius received honor and blessings for being a covenant keeper, and his story is not relayed to us through the Old Testament, but through the New Testament.

Don't Declare Covenant Obsolete and Lock It in the Past

My point is this: Covenant is a principle, a comprehensive set of God's promises for us and a lifestyle. It is not to be locked up in the past or disregarded as an obsolete Old Testament concept (if there is such a thing). Covenant is the way of Christ for your life and mine. The blessings of covenant can be yours today, but only if you receive them.

If you want to understand covenant in our day, examine how it operated in the lives of Ruth, Naomi and Boaz in the Old Testament: Naomi and her husband, Elimelech, were Israelites who were forced by famine to move with their two sons from Bethlehem to the land of Moab.[3] Mahlon, Naomi's eldest son, and his brother Kilion were far from Judah, so circumstances forced them to choose and marry wives from among the Moabites.

Circumstances changed 10 years later when Naomi lost her husband, Elimelech, and both of her sons died as well. When Naomi learned that God had removed the famine from Judah, she decided to go back home. All she had left were two daughters-in-law, and they were not obligated to her in any way after the death of their husbands. Naomi and her daughters-in-law left the place where they had been living and stopped on the road that would take them back to Judah.

Naomi told her daughters-in-law, "You do not have to go with me. Go back and live with your mothers. Find husbands from among your own people and be happy."[4] Then she blessed and kissed each of them as they wept. At first, neither one was willing to leave Naomi and they said they would return to Judah with her. In the end, Orpah decided to remain in Moab where her chances of finding a husband would be good. Ruth, however, had received more than her husband's name during their 10-year marriage. She also formed a lifelong covenant relationship with her mother-in-law and the God she saw in her life.

God Deal with Me If Anything Ever Separates Us

Even though Mahlon, the man who bound them together in the natural, was dead, Ruth knew she could not leave Naomi. She thought, *I want to stay with this woman because I have discovered God in her.* The obstacles didn't matter to her: Every means of financial support was gone since her husband, brother-in-law, and father-in-law had died. The odds that she would be able to marry an Israelite man were virtually nonexistent given her Moabite heritage. Such mixed marriages with descendants of ancient enemy nations were generally frowned upon. None of this mattered to Ruth. She turned to her mother-in-law and said something that had to have been inspired by God:

> Don't urge me to leave you or to turn back from you. Where you go I will go, and where you stay I will stay. Your people will be my people and your God my God. Where you die I will die, and there I will be buried. May the LORD deal with me, be it ever so severely, if anything but death separates you and me.[5]

Ruth's declaration to Naomi is the ultimate example of covenant identification with another person. The closest thing we see to this in the Old Testament is the relationship between David and Jonathan. This covenant declaration is considered the divine model for the intimate relationship and commitment between husbands and wives, and even the covenant relationship between God and those who serve Him.

Ruth Was Determined to Be Part of Naomi's Life

Naomi and Ruth were inseparable because Ruth was determined to be part of Naomi's life. What would happen in the Church if brothers and sisters in Christ also exhibited this same determination to walk together and allow nothing to separate them from God's presence and from one another? You know the answer—nothing could stop us!

Do you ever go back to where you were because you have lost something? Do you stop serving just because you have lost something? Where is your heart in the final analysis? Are you committed to serving the Lord no matter what comes and goes? Are you "in it for the money," or "in it for the benefits," or are you in this for the sake of covenant love? Before we go on, let me say that if you put yourself in the position to say, "I am determined and committed to serve the Lord at all costs," then I can tell you that God will take care of you and preserve your eternal destiny.

God does not take care of His children on a part-time basis because He is not a part-time father. He gives His complete attention to His children. If we respond to our Father, He will respond to us. Sometimes we have to be like Ruth and say to the Lord, "Don't tell me to leave. Don't ask me to go back. I refuse to turn back. My focus remains upon You—with all of my body, soul and spirit."

Many times, God wants to see if we are willing to follow Him without turning back. Ruth told Naomi, "Don't tell me to leave you or turn back." Then she said something that Jesus Christ said to the Church, "I am

Covenant doesn't abandon, even in the face of failure, an occasion of sin or personal weakness.

not going to leave you nor forsake you." This is covenant commitment in action: People in covenant with one another do not abandon each other when things get difficult. That is the difference between fair-weather friends and covenant friends. You can have the benefits of covenant right now as long as you are willing to commit to covenant relationships and not turn back if it takes you into stormy weather tomorrow.

It Is Not in God's Nature to Abandon His Children

God cannot and will not abandon us. His very nature as the author of covenant and the essence of truth and righteousness stands behind His eternal promises. Jesus, our Good Shepherd, ever lives to intercede to God the Father on our behalf.[6] He is our deliverer and redeemer. It is not in His nature to abandon His children. He imparted this same "gathering and keeping" spirit of a shepherd to us through the Holy Spirit so we can relate to one another in true covenant relationship.

That means that God ordained His people to relate to one another with the same stability, unchanging commitment and grace with which He relates to us. When we attach strings to our love, get offended and then abandon one another, we can be sure that God had nothing to do with our actions. No matter how hard we try to justify abandonment, or argue that covenant breaking can be condoned, it is not of God.

I've learned that none of us are where we are supposed to be in Christ. In other words, we all have a long way to go to be conformed to His image. Most of us are constantly learning spiritually, and some of us are more spiritual than others in the sense that we are learning faster or pressing into God's presence more earnestly. As a pastor and church leader, I've had to learn that sometimes God wants us to take our time and let other people in our lives catch up to us spiritually. If we don't obey His gentle leadings, we can allow spiritual ego to destroy us. This happens when we begin to think we are too deep and too spiritual for everyone around us. This kind of attitude can easily lead us to abandon people when God commands us to stay in covenant relationship.

Jesus knew in His wisdom that His disciples were young in the things of the Spirit. At times He had to rebuke them in a way that was strong enough to correct, but gentle enough to preserve their fragile faith. Paul the apostle also knew there were some things he could not share with the believers. He said:

> Brothers, I could not address you as spiritual but as worldly—mere infants in Christ. I gave you milk, not solid food, for you were not yet ready for it. Indeed, you are still not ready. You are still worldly. For since there is jealousy and quarreling among you, are you not worldly? Are you not acting like mere men?[7]

The Bible says when Ruth made her covenant statement to Naomi, she immediately realized her daughter-in-law could not be persuaded to turn away. Her heart was set and her mind was made up. With that settled, they began their journey to Bethlehem.

Ruth Exchanged Her Citizenship and Identity for Naomi's

Ruth was so focused and determined to walk in covenant that she was willing to drop her citizenship and identity to take on those of Naomi. Can you genuinely make that kind of commitment in a God-given covenant relationship? (It should be understood you cannot and should not enter into such a relationship with everybody—even in the Church!) If you can, then you are ready to receive the benefits of covenant as well.

This kind of covenant relationship is the absolute cure for chronic jealousy, criticism, backbiting, gossip and betrayal in the Body of Christ. It puts a permanent block on division in the local body, because its members absolutely and categorically refuse to be separated by rumor, innuendo, accusation or *even genuine wrongs*! Covenant doesn't abandon, even in the face of failure, an occasion of sin or personal weakness. Covenant causes us to embrace, forgive, restore and communicate with transparency whether things are going well or terribly. It is God's prescription for health in His Body on Earth.

From the moment Ruth made covenant with Naomi, a supernatural transfer and impartation of wisdom, virtue and spiritual heritage began to take place in a new way. The differences between them simply had no power to separate them: Naomi was old enough to be Ruth's mother, but she was as close to Ruth as a sister. Naomi was an Israelite descended from the tribe of Judah and Ruth was a Moabite, one of the traditional enemies of the Israelites that were distantly related to Abraham through Lot.

Boaz Kept Covenant and Triggered a Supernatural Blessing

The book of Ruth describes the beautiful way that God personally orchestrated Ruth's meeting with Boaz and their subsequent courtship and marriage. For his part, Boaz proved that he was a covenant keeper when he quickly offered help and support to his relative, Naomi, through Ruth. Then he took the ultimate step of covenant relationship when he went to the elders of Bethlehem and offered to perform the duties of a covenantal

redeemer kinsman by purchasing back all of the lands and property of Elimelech, Mahlon and Kilion. What he did next literally
triggered a supernatural blessing by the elders of his city:

> I have also acquired Ruth the Moabitess, Mahlon's widow,
> as my wife, in order to maintain the name of the dead with
> his property, so that his name will not disappear from
> among his family or from the town records. Today you are
> witnesses!" Then the elders and all those at the gate said,
> "We are witnesses. May the LORD make the woman who is
> coming into your home like Rachel and Leah, who togeth-
> er built up the house of Israel. May you have standing in
> Ephrathah and be famous in Bethlehem. Through the off-
> spring the LORD gives you by this young woman, may your
> family be like that of Perez, whom Tamar bore to Judah."[8]

First, Ruth made a lifelong covenant of love with her mother-in-law, Naomi. This brought her to Bethlehem and positioned
her for a divine appointment with Boaz, another covenant-keeping servant of God. Then Boaz honored the covenant between
Naomi and Ruth by treating Ruth as if she were an honored
member of his family line. He again kept covenant with Naomi's
deceased family members by taking on their debts as his own
and redeeming all of their land for Naomi. Thirdly, he honored
the principles of covenant by making a covenant of marriage
with Ruth and pledging before witnesses to raise up sons in the
name of Mahlon and Elimilech to preserve their family name.

Covenant-Keeping Positions You for Covenant Blessings

The covenant-keeping actions of Boaz positioned Ruth and
himself to receive God's covenant blessings and be remembered

forever. The elders responded by pronouncing a covenant blessing over Boaz and Ruth that was normally reserved only for
devout Israelites who were directly descended from Abraham
through Judah. The fruits of their prophetic covenant blessing
over Boaz and Ruth can be seen every time we speak of David,
their great-grandson, or read the lineage of Christ recorded in
the Gospels.[9]

The Lord remembered Ruth, the Moabite covenant keeper,
and her covenant-keeping husband, Boaz, and because of
covenant, God included this Moabite woman in the line of the
Messiah through David. The way you can receive the benefits of
covenant today is to begin to *keep* covenant today.

When I was growing up, I made it a point to spend time
with people who were older and wiser than I was so I could gain
knowledge and wisdom. Most of the young people my age were
too busy trying to have a good time, but I had been transformed by an encounter with God. I wanted the anointing of
God in my life, so I spent time with people who could help me
reach my goal. Once in a while these individuals would sit me
down and say, "Now let me talk to you, son," and they would
explain things to me about God and His kingdom. Little did I
know that those times of covenant sharing would impact my
life.

Many of us short-circuit the flow of covenant benefits to
our lives by listening to the distracting, wearying whispers of
Satan. I can guarantee you that if you begin to walk in covenant
with God and with other members of His Body, the Church, the
enemy will begin to whisper to you, "This sure is taking a long
time. Look at all the years you've spent reaching this point. Do
you really have anything to show for it? After all, what's in it for
you? If I were you, I would turn around and go back. I wouldn't
put up with this waiting and serving business any longer."

It Never Pays to "Go Back" on Your Covenant Commitment to God

Thank God for the Holy Spirit who also speaks softly to our hearts, saying, "Don't be weary. You only have a short way to go. Don't quit now, I'll be with you every step of the way. Don't stop now. You have invested too much time, energy, finances and hope in this precious dream to give up now."

It never pays to "go back" anyway, because once you experience the benefits of God's covenants, nothing else will do! The other reason is that when you go back, when you break covenant, God still upholds His part of the covenant. He will pursue you with gentle love and conviction to woo you back into His fold where you belong. We may try to abandon God, but He always keeps covenant. He will not abandon us.

We have to position ourselves to receive from God, and that never happens merely by wishing for it or by apathetically watching others seek Him. There is no room for "spectator Christianity" in the Church, but that has become our chief characteristic. The only way to receive the benefits of covenant is to make and keep covenant with God and man. That requires action on our part.

Most people are afraid to enter into close relationships with people in their local church because of the two great fears of life: rejection and failure. I wish we could understand that covenant is God's solution and deliverance from those fears. Let me ask you this: How would you feel if someone told you, "I am in covenant with you. We are together for life. We are going to serve God together"? How would you feel with that kind of reassurance surrounding you? I have a feeling you would be ready to attempt the impossible with that kind of unconditional love and support behind you. That is God's intention!

God Can Do Anything When There
Is Covenant in a Local Church

God's promises to you are sure, and He will never reject you or fail you. People may fail, but within the bonds of covenant, there is abundant room for reconciliation, forgiveness, healing and fresh starts. Do you know what God can do when there is covenant in a local church? He can do anything!

If a local church body is in covenant, there is nothing that church can't do. The members of that church are like the members of a physical body. When I look at my body, I know that my head is "in covenant" with my nose for the purpose of survival and proper functioning. Even though my head may not like my nose during hay fever season, it is still in covenant. (My head knows that the moment I decide to remove my offensive nose, I will disfigure myself. So they are in covenant.) My heart is in covenant with both of them as well, and so is my stomach. The body needs the heart and the stomach, and it also needs my feet. Each part is necessary in its proper place and function. So should it be in the covenant community called the local church.

If God can get hold of a local church body that is united and committed to one another just as they are committed to Him and His purposes, there is nothing He cannot do through them. It is time for us to walk in covenant unity and reap the benefits of covenant power in our towns, communities, cities and nation.

Covenant is so powerful that it crosses the lines of the impossible into the miraculous. How else could a Moabite widow with no future become the wife of a wealthy Israelite man and give birth to a son who would become part of the line of the Messiah! Where there is covenant, love covers an abundance of sin and past mistakes. It all begins with the blood covenant of Christ that He cut on the Cross. From there, He takes us into a lifelong covenant of caring commitment to brothers and sisters in our local church that makes life an adventure of faith.

Jesus was in covenant with Peter, and even though Peter publicly denied Jesus three times, the Lord refused to let Peter remain in his shame. When He met Peter again after the Resurrection, Peter remembered that he had made and broken a commitment to the Lord. He immediately fixed it through repentance and received forgiveness and total restoration through covenant. In covenant, Jesus prayed for Peter in advance, knowing he would break covenant and fail.

God used the principles of covenant to restore Peter to the point where the same man, who once denied Jesus when challenged by one woman, was able to stand publicly before thousands to boldly preach the gospel. This same man who failed was able to endure the pain of a whip and the terror of prison to continue preaching the gospel. This is what a supernatural covenant with God can do to normal, everyday followers of Christ. It all begins with our personal commitment to Jesus Christ, the Mediator of our better covenant with God.

Notes
1. See James 1:22.
2. 3 John 1:1-6, italics mine.
3. The Moabites were the descendants of Lot's oldest son, who was conceived in incest with his eldest daughter (see Genesis 19:29-37).
4. My illustrative paraphrase of Ruth 1:8,9.
5. Ruth 1:16,17.
6. See Hebrews 7:25.
7. 1 Corinthians 3:1-3
8. Ruth 4:10-12.
9. See Matthew 1:5; Luke 3:32.

challenges for COVENANT thinking

SECTION FOUR

how to renew and preserve
COVENANT

CHAPTER 11

Keeping Bonds Fresh

Every time Americans stand together and recite the "Pledge of Allegiance," they are renewing and preserving a national covenant that was established more than 200 years ago. When 70,000 sports fans stand to sing the national anthem and salute the American flag, they are renewing and preserving that same covenant.

Jesus said, "Any kingdom divided against itself will be ruined, and a house divided against itself will fall."[1] That goes for any family home or local church body as well. So what happens when offense comes? What remedy do we have when a member of the family, a church member or a church leader betrays a trust or the whole group becomes splintered over a divisive issue or crisis? That all depends on whether or not they walk in covenant together.

What is the secret for passing down to our children and grandchildren all the things we've learned about the Christian life? The answer is found in covenant. All of us need to learn how to respond to covenant in times of disagreement, strife or crisis. Covenants are to be obeyed, kept and renewed, or strengthened. Without the stability and guidance they provide, people tend to respond to convenience or the path of least resistance instead of truth and righteousness.

Covenant relationships in local church bodies are weakened when people enter covenant selfishly, motivated primarily by a desire to find support and healing for their own personal needs. Covenant always demands a two-way relationship, personal responsibility and commitment. The reality is that most covenant organizations, from the family unit to the Church, have covenant members who don't understand the mutual commitment aspect of covenant life.

These problems and weaknesses, combined with the daily stresses and challenges of being and dealing with flawed human beings, require us to renew and preserve our covenant relationships and commitments on a regular basis. By renew, I mean that we "make like new, restore to freshness, restore to existence, revive, do again, or begin again."[2] We preserve covenant when we keep it—or our covenant brothers and sisters—"safe from injury, harm, or destruction; keep alive, intact, or free from decay; to keep or save from decomposition."[3]

Is the Renewal or Preservation of Covenant in the Bible?

By my count, the *NIV* of the Bible contains 297 references to covenant in 271 verses, spanning both the Old and the New

Testaments. For the sake of perspective, I've listed just 12 things the Bible says about how God and His people renew or preserve covenant:

1. Moses *renewed* the covenant by *reading* it aloud before the people, by symbolically *sprinkling them with the blood* of the sacrifice, and by requiring the Israelites to *corporately and verbally pledge* themselves to keep it in Exodus 24:7 (italics mine). King Josiah followed the same general pattern in 2 Chronicles 34:31 as well.

2. The Israelites were to *celebrate* the perpetual covenant of the Sabbath as a sign of God's covenant (Exodus 31:16,17, italics mine).

3. God Himself *renewed* His covenant with His people *by doing signs and wonders* before them in Exodus 34:10 (italics mine).

4. The Israelites were commanded to "keep" or *preserve* the covenant by *obeying* God's commands in Deuteronomy 7:11,12 (italics mine).

5. Moses reminded the Israelites to *ask about God's deeds and faithfulness* to their forefathers, and to *recount their covenant history* of faith in Deuteronomy 4:31-40 (italics mine).

6. King Asa *rebuilt and repaired what had fallen down* in 2 Chronicles 15:8 (italics mine).

7. Under King Asa's leadership, the Israelites also renewed their ancient covenant with God when they "*entered into a covenant to seek the LORD*, the God of their fathers, with all their heart and soul" in 2 Chronicles 15:12 (italics mine).

8. King David renewed his covenant with God after committing adultery and murder by *confessing his sins*, by

asking for mercy and forgiveness, by asking God to *"renew a steadfast spirit"* within him, and by *offering the sacrifices of a broken spirit;* a broken and contrite heart" in Psalm 51 (italics mine).

9. The prophet Nehemiah *interceded* for his people day and night to God, and *vicariously confessed their sins* against God in Nehemiah 1:6 (italics mine).

10. God's timeless path of restoration for His people appears in 2 Chronicles 7:14: "If my people, who are called by my name, will *humble themselves* and *pray* and *seek my face* and *turn from their wicked ways,* then will I hear from heaven and will forgive their sin and will heal their land" (italics mine).

11. God promised "an everlasting name" to men who would *"choose what pleases Me"* and *"hold fast* to My covenant" in Isaiah 56:4 (italics mine).

12. God Himself revealed that He preserves His covenants with men with His promise that *neither His Spirit nor His Word would "depart from the mouths" of His people,* their children, or their descendants forever in Isaiah 59:21 (italics mine).

We have established that the renewal and preservation or keeping of covenant is in the Bible, but most people still have serious doubts that they have ever broken a covenant. Most of the time, these doubts come because we don't understand what covenant is and what it is not.

The Covenant We Love to Break
We need to renew a covenant whenever we have broken a covenant agreement in some way or another, or when we allow it

to be forgotten or laid aside. One of the most commonly broken covenants in the Church is the covenant of tithes and offerings described in the book of Malachi. We don't lose our salvation when we fail to give tithes and offerings to the Lord, but we will reap the consequences of breaking covenant with God.

Such actions will cause God to lift His blessings and protection from our lives. The Bible says, "But remember the LORD your God, for it is he who gives you the ability to produce wealth, and so confirms his covenant, which he swore to your forefathers, as it is today."[4]

He is the source of our ability to get wealth and the ultimate protector of all of the resources, gifts, abilities and health that we have. These things quickly disappear once God steps back to let us have our own way. We can count on it because it is in God's Book. When we hold back our tithes and offerings, it amounts to robbing God and putting our own curse upon our pocket.

Israel in the time of Malachi had wandered far from the Lord, even though they thought they were very religious. When God told them, "Ever since the time of your forefathers you have turned away from my decrees and have not kept them. Return to me, and I will return to you," their response was, "How are we to return?"[5] This is the same as asking, "How can we renew our covenant with You?" God's answer is just as valid today as it was in Malachi's day:

> "Will a man rob God? Yet you rob me. But you ask, 'How do we rob you?' In tithes and offerings. You are under a curse—the whole nation of you—because you are robbing me. Bring the whole tithe into the storehouse, that there may be food in my house. Test me in this," says the LORD Almighty, "and see if I will not throw open the flood-gates of heaven and pour out so much blessing that you

will not have room enough for it. I will prevent pests from devouring your crops, and the vines in your fields will not cast their fruit," says the LORD Almighty. "Then all the nations will call you blessed, for yours will be a delightful land," says the LORD Almighty.[6]

The Lord Wants Covenant Faithfulness

God doesn't need our money; He owns all of the gold, diamonds, silver, platinum in the earth and "the cattle on a thousand hills."[7] God wants our covenant faithfulness, and that specifically includes tithes and offerings.

Any money or resources that we put into our untithing pocket will seem to drop away through holes that we never noticed before. Whatever we sow just won't seem to grow, causing us to sow much and reap little. Even though we may work an extra job or longer hours to get ahead, we only seem to fall farther behind. Why? We are not in covenant with God in our finances.

If you choose not to acknowledge the fact that it is God who gives you the power to get wealth, then your Source simply allows you to do it on your own. That is a miserable prospect at best.

It is easy to dismiss the importance of tithes and offerings if we feel we are just giving our money to the preacher or to some corporate church entity that seems to have no needs. The truth is that even though God uses people to administrate the earthly use of that money, we are actually giving our honor, respect and a part of ourselves back to Him—regardless of how people use or misuse the money given. He will reward us for our gifts, and He will reward them for the way they use or misuse His tithes.

Many Believers Have Never Been
Taught to Walk in Covenant

The sad truth is that generation after generation of children grow up with a curse upon them because their fathers did not operate in or teach them about the covenant blessings of God.

Many godly families in this situation are doing their best in Christ to live right, but the problem is that they have never been taught how to walk in covenant with God. It is time for us to return to God's Word and find out what He really has to say about money, poverty and abundant supply. God is well able and more than willing to change circumstances for any of His children. It is part of the covenant. The root problem is broken covenant.

This covenant can quickly be renewed by repenting of past mistakes and correcting the problem today. Begin to faithfully give your tithes—I recommend that you make it the first check you write when you receive your paycheck or some other kind of income. Begin to give gifts over and above your tithe as well, and test God's promise as He commanded us in Malachi. Plant your financial seed of faith into the soil of His promises and watch to see Him multiply blessings back into your life. He is faithful beyond measure or hope.

When you renew the covenant in your finances, you are planting seeds in the Kingdom, and you are planting seeds for a harvest in the life of your children and your children's children! I recommend that you sow good seeds today for your children to reap tomorrow.

The tithe and offering is directly linked to God's chosen method of confirming His covenant with His people right in front of their enemies. When we dismiss the tithe as legalism from the Old Testament, we miss the whole point of tithes and offerings. The tithe predates the Law given to Moses on Mount Sinai—it isn't a legal precedent set in ancient Israel; it is a spiritual principle established in one of the earliest chapters in the Bible.[8]

The Heart of Covenant Living—Give Him Our All!

We need to rediscover how to activate God's promises through faith-filled giving of tithes and generous offerings with thanksgiving. We need to turn the key of joyous giving and harvest the benefits of the Law of sowing and reaping. This isn't a get-rich-quick scheme or a blab it/grab it teaching. It is the heart of covenant living to consider all that we have, all that we are and all that we ever hope to be is the property of God. This is what it means to give all to Him.

Tithes and offerings are not merely pre-Christian Levitical law as some argue. They are God's solution for financial need and abundant supply for the expansion of His covenant. As covenant-keeping children of our covenant-keeping God, it is our privilege to give our way out of debt and into financial blessings. The reason He blesses us is so that we can be a blessing and confirm God's covenant to our generation and the generations to come.

When we break covenant with God, happiness quickly begins to fade and everything in our lives will begin to fall apart. As covenant people, God's blessings flow through us like water through a garden hose to openly confirm His covenant before the world. When we break covenant, our actions turn off the tap at the source and God's flow of blessings trickles to a stop no matter what we do.

One of the men in my congregation had great promise and potential for success in the business world. I watched and encouraged him to pursue his destiny in the Lord. At my invitation, we met and discussed his business plan several years ago, and I told him, "You are going to go places." I said that with the understanding that he would continue to walk in the covenant principles he had learned from God's Word. When his business took off, he started breaking covenant in his business practices and conduct. I wasn't surprised to learn recently that he ended up on the streets and no one knows where he is now.

Covenant Renewal Under the New Covenant

Jesus Christ Himself gave us the strongest and most important method for renewing and preserving His covenant in the Church when He instituted holy Communion on the night He was betrayed.[9] It is one of the few things Jesus commanded His followers to observe in scrupulous detail, yet we have managed in most cases to rob it of most of its power. As you review His words, look for the earmarks of covenant in His instructions:

> For I received from the Lord what I also passed on to you: The Lord Jesus, on the night he was betrayed, took bread, and when he had given thanks, he broke it and said, "This is my body, which is for you; *do this in remembrance of me.*" In the same way, after supper he took the cup, saying, "This cup is the new covenant in my blood; do this, whenever you drink it, in remembrance of me." *For whenever you eat this bread and drink this cup, you proclaim the Lord's death until he comes.* Therefore, whoever eats the bread or drinks the cup of the Lord in an unworthy manner *will be guilty of sinning against the body and blood of the Lord.* A man ought to examine himself before he eats of the bread and drinks of the cup. For anyone who

eats and drinks without recognizing the body of the Lord eats and drinks judgment on himself. That is why many among you are weak and sick, and a number of you have fallen asleep.[10]

Every time we gather together in Christ's name to share Communion, we are renewing and preserving the blood covenant of Jesus Christ that saves us, heals us, preserves us, unites us, keeps us and restores us to eternal fellowship with God our Father. This is the Lord's prescription for broken, weakened, fractured or strained covenant relationships.

It is a fact that you and I cannot have true communion unless we are willing to forgive one another, laying aside every grudge, hurt or grievance in His name.[11] The apostle John told us not to claim that we love God unless we also love our brothers.[12] It can't be said any plainer than that.

Covenant Life Produces Supernatural Growth and Unity

The first-century Church actively demonstrated the power of fellowship around the Communion table when they "broke bread in their homes and ate together with glad and sincere hearts."[13] This is covenant life in action, and it is powerful. Perhaps this is why the church at Jerusalem grew so quickly. The believers constantly renewed and preserved their new covenant in Christ. They set their central focus on their Savior, and they were of one spirit, one mind and one accord.

These are the fruits of our blood covenant in Christ. Let me assure you that the same fruits will grow every time you plant the seeds of covenant living and servanthood into your home, your family, your business and your ministry to others.

Another way we preserve covenant is to maintain or keep godly attitudes and perspectives. Some of us we think we are better than other people. Like the Pharisees of Jesus' day, we think we are too special to relate to lesser people, considering ourselves to be God's gift to the world. It is more like we are God's problem children.

The Lord can't work with independent contractors, because the Kingdom is a family covenant affair. We are in this together or we aren't in it at all! Anyone who has a problem with this will have to take it up with the Boss. A better-than-thou attitude quickly negates the benefits of covenant in our lives, and may even cause other people to stumble. That puts us squarely in opposition to God Himself, and that is not a safe place to be.[14]

A better-than-thou attitude quickly negates the benefits of covenant in our lives.

Sometimes, preserving covenant means we have to tell the truth even when it puts us at risk! There are two times in David's life when he committed sins that caused men to approach him with the uncomfortable truth that God had found him out.

The first was when Nathan the prophet came to David and confronted him about his adultery with Bathsheba and the murder of her husband, Uriah. These sins amounted to betrayal of the worst sort because Uriah was one of "Thirty Mighty Men" described in great detail in the Bible. He was loyal to the death to David his king, and it was his loyalty that made it impossible for David to hide his sin.

When Nathan approached King David, he described the crime against Uriah in parable form and David instantly said,

"The man who did this deserves to die!" Nathan answered, "You are the man!"[15] Nathan had to obey God even though by the customs of that day, King David had the power to order him killed immediately. Nathan kept covenant by telling the truth, and David renewed his covenant through repentance.

The second incident happened when David displeased the Lord by numbering or taking a census of the fighting men in his kingdom. God Himself confronted David this time, but He sent Gad the seer to the king to deliver the bad news about his choice of punishments for his sin. The resulting judgment caused the death of 70,000 men, and nearly resulted in the destruction of Jerusalem.[16]

The Blood of the Covenant Covers Every Sin

When we stand in the presence of God as believers, covenant partners with Jesus Christ, God not only sees us as forgiven and cleansed of all the sins of the past, but He also sees that covenant blood actively working on our behalf in the present and in the future! Jesus' blood has power because He perfectly fulfilled God's purposes within the boundaries of every covenant in existence. By His obedience, He literally cut a new and greater blood covenant on the Cross. Wherever God sees the blood of His Son's covenant, He moves heaven and Earth to honor it. Why? Because He is the covenant-keeping God of eternity.

Covenant is a vow. Most of us are unfamiliar with vows, but covenant is a solemn commitment that we make with God, other individuals, ourselves, our immediate family or with relatives. Covenant commitments are very serious in God's eyes, so we must keep our covenant commitments. Jesus made it clear that we must renew our covenant with Him daily. He said: "If anyone would come after me, he must deny himself and take up his cross daily and follow me."[17]

We have taken covenant for granted for so long that, in many local church bodies, betrayal has almost become the norm for personal relationships among their members. It is time for all of us to crucify our pride and selfishness on the cross of Christ and follow Him into true covenant love. The cure for our sickness is to repent and return to the covenant life of God. Where can you find better covenant relationship than in the Body of Christ? God's intent was that we all become one family and one people through our blood covenant in Christ.

God Used My Failure to Teach Me How to Preserve Covenant

I have many friends from many nations, but one of my dearest and best friends lives in the Bahamas. Dr. Myles Munroe and I are very close, and we are identical in every way except for our physical height. We think alike to the extent that from time to time, he and I will "go at it" or bicker and verbally wrestle with one another over various topics like blood brothers.

One time I decided that I had had enough, and I just looked at him and told him what I thought. My words definitely weren't kind, but I thought at the time that my anger justified my actions. When I finally stopped long enough to receive a response, Dr. Munroe simply looked at me and smiled.

That was not what I had expected. I thought he would roar back with his own tirade. But my precious brother did not do that. Myles refused to acknowledge my foolishness. Instead, he looked me in the eye and said with unmistakable sincerity,

"Kingsley, you know I love you. I hear what you are saying. That is the way you feel, but I don't feel the way you feel."

The Way of Covenant

It became apparent that I had allowed the opinions of other people to affect my attitude toward Dr. Munroe. I began to realize that Myles had different kinds of relationships with different people, and the people whose complaints I'd entertained actually did not know Myles Munroe that well. They were not in covenant with Myles, nor were they in covenant with me—they were acquaintances. I was wrong to act that way toward my covenant brother anyway, but I was also wrong to allow the critical comments of an acquaintance to influence my covenant relationship with a longtime covenant brother. I had to repent to Myles for my conduct and of course he was quick to forgive me and embrace my neck. That is the way of covenant.

God used that incident to show me that I should never endanger or spoil the special things He has placed in my life. Dr. Myles Munroe is a covenant brother and a gift from God in my life. He has proven to me that his love for me has nothing to do with what I have achieved or what reputation I may have. Myles loves me for me, in the same way the Lord extends unconditional love to me. Dr. Munroe is a friend whom I can call upon at any time. I know he genuinely cares for me, and he knows I feel the same way about him. I thank God for using Myles to show me the kind of true love that is available only in the bonds of covenant, and how I was to renew and preserve my covenant with my brother.

If you see or experience true covenant in your life, you will always find these things embedded and intertwined in your relationships: truth, honesty, sacrifice, sincerity and sharing. You cannot be in covenant without them. Most people prefer relationships of convenience because it takes sacrifice and commitment to keep and maintain covenant. There is no covenant without sacrifice, because at times you have to go out of your way to fulfill covenant.

Finally, I want to share with you how the Lord instructed me to include my children in our family covenant. Although my wife and I tried to model and instruct our children in covenant principles from their earliest moments of understanding, I felt led to do something more once they came of age. I called them to a very important family meeting and told them: "From this day on, you will be included when any major decision must be made which affects you or this household. I want you to know what Daddy and Mommy are doing, so from now on you are to be included in our discussions concerning all important matters."

Why did I do this? I knew my children would never forget that day in their lives. It was a godly "rite of passage" into a new level of covenant understanding and responsibility. I embraced and kissed them, and welcomed them into the covenant of the family. Yes, they were still children, but it was time for them to share in our respect for the family covenant as well as in its blessings. I encourage you to ask God how He wants you to include your family members in your covenant life. If you can teach your children the principles of covenant early in their lives, they will not depart from those truths to live ungodly lives and break covenant later on.

Notes
1. Luke 11:17.
2. Word definition for "renew" adapted from *Merriam-Webster's Collegiate Dictionary*, 10th ed., s.v. "renew."
3. Ibid, s.v. "preserve."

4. Deuteronomy 8:18.

5. Malachi 3:7.

6. Malachi 3:8-12.

7. See Psalm 50:7-14. This passage illustrates the danger of breaking covenant with God, as well as His mercy toward us when we repent.

8. See Genesis 14:17-20; Hebrews 7:1-10.

9. See Luke 22:15-22.

10. 1 Corinthians 11:23-30.

11. See Matthew 5:23,24.

12. See 1 John 3:14,15,17,18; 4:20,21.

13. Acts 2:46.

14. See Matthew 18:6-10; Luke 17:1-4.

15. See 2 Samuel 12:1-7.

16. See 2 Samuel 24:10-12,15,16.

17. Luke 9:23. (Note that Jesus wasn't saying we need to get "saved" daily, we just need to renew our covenant of discipleship with Him and then take up our cross or *act* accordingly.)

the power of covenant in a new
MILLENNIUM

CHAPTER 12

Changes on the Horizon

Change seems to be the only fixed characteristic of life on Earth in the new millennium. Everything outside of the kingdom of God is in a constant state of flux or transition, and much of what we consider to be His kingdom is in transition as well. He is shaking and transforming His Church on an astonishing scale.

We can count on this fact: No matter what we encounter this year or 100 years from now, God will place His divine template of covenant right in the middle of our lives to bring heaven's stability into our unstable world. Covenant describes the full range of God's promises to and relationships and interactions with mankind, and it is more vital to us today than it has ever been.

A firm foundation is even important when building a house on land that is stable, dry and supported by substrata of limestone, granite or even sandstone. It is crucial when you have to build a structure on the sinking soil of New Orleans or in the sinking city of Venice, Italy.

God has called His covenant people to build a kingdom of power and a city of light in the middle of our sinking society and darkening moral climate. The only way we can accomplish this is by serving, working and sacrificing together as a covenant people, bound together by the blood of the Lamb and His finished work on the Cross.

There are seven reasons I believe covenant relationships and God's covenant principles will be crucial to us in our new millennium. They are not new, but they illustrate why covenant is even more vital to us as we begin a new era marked by greater separation of human society in general from God's Word and will.

Seven Vital Reasons Covenant Is Crucial in the Millennium of Change

1. *Covenant Creates and Preserves the Strength of Unity.*
   Covenant qualifies us for tapping into the strength, unity and staying power of the threefold cord relationship. Solomon, a wise man, devoted a number of verses in Ecclesiastes to the power and virtue of unity among brethren:

   Two are better than one, because they have a good return for their work: If one falls down, his friend can help him up. But pity the man who falls and has no one to help him up! Also, if two lie down together, they will keep warm. But how can one keep warm alone? Though one may be overpowered, two can defend themselves. *A cord of three strands is not quickly broken.*[1]

The strength of three-stranded unity is vital to our covenant community of faith. We need that kind of strength to succeed, since we are sent to bring light to a nation marked by growing antagonism against God's people and hot resentment over any influence we exert on society.

2. *Covenant Harnesses the Power of Unity Among Men to the Power of God.*
Covenant not only musters up the power of human unity, but more importantly, it submits that force of unity to the plan and will of God. This releases the resources of heaven on our behalf to help us achieve God's covenant purposes for each generation.

God invested us with the capacity to exponentially multiply our power through unity. Evidently, this ability was imparted to us when God made us in His likeness and image. It was this capacity that caused Him to confound the languages of man early in our history after godless men united to make their own name apart from God:

Then they said, "Come, let us build ourselves a city, with a tower that reaches to the heav-

ens, so that we may make a name for ourselves and not be scattered over the face of the
whole earth." But the LORD came down to see
the city and the tower that the men were
building. The LORD said, "If as one people
speaking the same language they have begun
to do this, then nothing they plan to do will
be impossible for them. Come, let us go down
and confuse their language so they will not
understand each other." So the LORD scattered them from there over all the earth, and
they stopped building the city.[2]

The fact that God acted to separate godless men thousands of years ago does not mean that He never intended to reunite us so we can use that power for His purposes! In fact, that is His exact intention. Under the
blood covenant of Christ and through the framework
of His Church, God intends to unite us in supernatural unity by His Spirit. In my opinion, that miracle is
scheduled for such a time as this.

3. *Covenant Is God's Most Powerful Evangelism Tool.*
   According to 1 Corinthians 13, the greatest of all gifts
   is love, for love never fails. Covenant love is the ultimate answer to a generation longing for belonging.
   Only the covenant love of God and His earthly family
   can overpower the attraction of street gangs who constantly recruit hurting young people seeking love and
   nurture outside of their dysfunctional homes. The love
   of Christ spans every ungodly thing that has divided
   mankind, and it has created a supernatural family that

possesses a love that cannot be matched or duplicated on earth. Covenant is the heavenly container for displaying God's love to the world through the Church.

4. *God Uses Covenant to Heal the Brokenhearted, Protect the Weak and Restore the Dysfunctional.*

Covenant is God's vehicle for delivering supernatural healing and restoration to the hurting people who have become unwilling by-products of a dysfunctional, self-destructive society. By God's design, His healing balm is packaged in the natural bodies and human hearts of His covenant people, the Church.

Our limitations and weakness as ordinary people showcase God's transforming power at work in our lives.[3] If anything can give hope to someone who is wounded, it is the light of God in the eyes of someone who was once wounded as they are.[4] This is the description of God's covenant family of sinners saved by grace.

5. *Covenant Is God's Original Seminary and School of Ministry in Seasons of Rapid Harvest.*

Covenant is the only way to raise up ministry and train believers for the work of the ministry fast enough in a season of rapid harvest. It allows the development of supernatural gifts to occur side by side with the development of godly character, loyalty and faithfulness.

The word "minister" has never referred to someone who is pulpit hungry. A minister is one who continues to wait like a waitress. To minister is to serve or make yourself available. That is something we have not come into yet. You see, the more you know, the more it humbles you to become a servant. We don't have the servant spirit yet. Unless you have a serving spirit, the glory of God cannot manifest in your life.

Covenant has a way of weeding out self-centered people and those who refuse to submit to authority of any kind. All of us have authority and submission issues to deal with in the course of our lives, but some people make their aim in life to rebel against everyone and everything that places limits and boundaries on their actions.

Some Christians who match that description get conformed to Christ's image by the grating, pride-breaking and loving pressures of covenant love and become great leaders with servant's hearts. Most quickly try to escape the influence and transparent atmosphere of covenant relationship because they are unable to bear its intimacy and openhearted submission of one to another.

> Covenant has a way of weeding out self-centered people.

6. *God Reveals His Power and Purpose to Nonbelievers by Publicly Confirming His Covenant with Believers.*
Covenant exists to confirm God's existence, power and love for mankind to every unbelieving generation. God openly blesses His people, and demonstrates how He transforms the lives of ordinary people to do extraordinary things in His name.

Every time He keeps His promises to His people, it sets them apart from those who do not live in covenant relationship with Him. The supernatural nature of the Church will become more and more apparent in this millennium as God cleanses and purifies His Bride to rise up in unprecedented unity, holiness and singleness of purpose.

7. *Covenant Creates Accountability and
    Keeps Us Moving Forward.*
    The book of Proverbs describes one of the most important dynamics of covenant life with these words: "As iron sharpens iron, so one man sharpens another."[5] When we are in covenant with others who know us well (and love us anyway), they can help keep us accountable for our actions while loving and caring for us unceasingly. This only works with covenant partners—people who share your total allegiance to God, to His Word and to the fulfillment of His purposes in the earth. In covenant, we share with one another many of the things God is saying to us individually. We confide our secret longings and divine prompting; and a week later or a year later, we confront one another to ask, "By the way, brother, what about that task God gave you last month or last year? Have you done anything that may hinder its completion?"

    Covenant keeps us from settling down, slowing down and stopping short of our individual and corporate callings in Christ. Although I have classified this as a category all of its own, it is closely related to the power and value of the threefold cord relationship. We need one another to reach our full potential in Christ.

    Covenant relationships should also stimulate our personal hunger to press deeper into God's presence.

The more time we spend with what my covenant brother Tommy Tenney calls "God chasers," the more likely we are to join and continue the chase as well. Nothing unifies and solidifies the bonds of love among Christians as effectively as times of corporate repentance, praise, worship and adoration of God. The more we focus on Him, the less important become all of the things that hinder and divide us at times.

If We Truly Know Him, We Will Be Truly Changed

It is vital that we *know* the Lord personally and experientially by seeking His face and waiting upon Him in worship, adoration, meditation and even silence at times. When we come into His presence, we are changed in a way that should be visible to those around us. The Bible says:

Now the Lord is the Spirit, and where the Spirit of the Lord is, there is freedom. And we, *who with unveiled faces all reflect the Lord's glory*, are being transformed into his likeness with ever-increasing glory, which comes from the Lord, who is the Spirit.[6]

If you are around nonchurch people very much, you will quickly learn that they have a keen discernment even in their unsaved state. A stone-cold sinner can always tell the difference in those who really know God and those who are just religious. That difference will become even more crucial as we move deeper into this new millennium and closer to the great harvest of the last days.

We have to *know Him* and *know one another* to follow Him into the unknown together. He is going to lead the entire Church into a new place, just as He once led the nation of Israel across the river Jordan into a promised land. Before God could effectively fulfill His promise to the descendants of Abraham, He had to transform them into a *covenant-based nation with a new identity and mind-set.*

He was going to take the Israelites to a place where they had never been before, and require them to do things they had never imagined. Had the first generation obeyed God, then the world would have witnessed the miraculous transformation of a nation of slaves into a nation of conquerors. In one stroke, He intended to transport them from being the tail to being the head; from being beneath Egypt's thumb to being above all of the nations and inhabitants of Canaan.

God Wants to Give the Church
a New Covenant Identity

The Church, as the spiritual people of God, has the same opportunity in this millennium as did Israel in Moses' day. We have known what it is to be the tail in American society: to be outcasts socially, politically and economically. At times, we have handled our earthly calling to be a "light to the nations"[7] as slaves instead of as kings and priests to our God. The Lord is out to transform the Church into a covenant-based spiritual nation with a new identity and mind-set!

Our unity and identity is not based on common programs, or shared ethnicity or socioeconomic backgrounds. It is based solely on the blood covenant of God established through the sacrificial death and resurrection of Jesus Christ. Regardless of our various understandings and convictions concerning end-time events and timetables, we all agree that Jesus is coming for a victorious Bride without spot or wrinkle.[8] That requires transformation, and so does the task of taking the gospel to every creature.

In the Church of Christ's covenant, it is common for people to point to a covenant believer and say, "Hey, do you remember that guy? He used to be the one of the biggest drug dealers and gangbangers in the area. I don't know what happened to him, but it had to be big." The covenant of God transforms everything about us because it is God's way of conforming or reshaping us to the image of Jesus Christ.

This explains why I keep hammering away at the subject of covenant. We can call it a hundred different things, and that is fine—as long as we don't discard covenant as irrelevant or unimportant in the Christian life. Covenant *is* the Christian life in Christ.

Six Ways God Uses the Instrumentality of Covenant

God uses the instrumentality of covenant to nurture us when we are young in the faith, to train us as we grow in maturity, and to prepare us to serve Him and operate in our gifts. He uses covenant to restore and renew us when we are wounded or broken in some way. Covenant becomes an impenetrable hedge of protection around us as brothers and sisters encircle us when we are under assault, whether it be spiritual, physical, financial or mental. And finally, the covenant of God and the covenant relationships it creates transform the corporate Body of Christ into an invincible weapon in the hands of God to destroy the works of the enemy in communities, nations and entire generations.

The power of covenant is essentially the power of revealing the mystery of God at work in us, the presence and work of "Christ in us, the hope of glory."[9] We have no greater calling than to stretch out into the unknown ahead of us in covenant love and unity, equipped with God's covenant promises, with the Good News of Jesus Christ. The task may seem impossible, but what may seem impossible to men is possible with our covenant-keeping God.

The journey to obedience that releases the power of covenant in your life begins each morning with a conscious decision. Each day you must deny yourself, pick up your cross of discipleship in Christ, and walk in His will as a covenant keeper and member of the kingdom of God on Earth.[10]

I prayed this prayer for you before this book ever went to press. Now I invite you to pray it to the Lord yourself and receive His answer in your life. If the Holy Spirit spoke to your heart as you read various portions of this book, allow this time in prayer to be your answer to His gentle voice and prompting:

Father, in the name of Jesus,

We thank You for Your great love, and the gift of life You gave us through Jesus, Your Son. Prepare us to look forward to great things. Transform and conform us, so we can press on and obey Your every command. We commit together to become a people of covenant— not only with You but also with our brothers and sisters.

Have Your way in our lives, and transform us into a covenant-based nation of kings and priests, a people invested with a new identity and mind-set. We commit ourselves to become members individually and together with a church of believers who understand covenant. May we walk in the spirit of covenant, with humility and love toward one another.

As we seek and serve You together, reveal to us Your heart and impart to us Your compassion for the weary, the outcast and the brokenhearted. By Your Spirit, cause us to be doers of Your Word rather than hearers only.

Lead us out of temptation and deliver us from evil as we walk together in obedience, and in transparent covenant love. We rejoice in the joy of Your presence. In Jesus' name we pray these things with thanksgiving and praise.

Amen.

Notes
1. Ecclesiastes 4:9-12, italics mine.
2. Genesis 11:4-8, italics mine.
3. See 2 Corinthians 4:7.
4. See 2 Corinthians 1:3-6.
5. Proverbs 27:17.
6. 2 Corinthians 3:17,18, italics mine.
7. See Isaiah 49:6,7.
8. See Ephesians 5:27.
9. See Colossians 1:27.
10. See Luke 9:23.

resources by
KINGSLEY FLETCHER

Books

I Have Seen the Kingdom
After two centuries of democracy and free will, has America lost sight of the biblical views held by her founders? Kingsley Fletcher shows how we can still tap into the glory of God through a renewed understanding of Kingdom principles.

Prayer and Fasting
Fasting and prayer will sharpen your expectancy so that when you ask, you expect to receive. This best-selling book is a practical guide to a lifestyle of effective prayer and fasting, explaining preparation, purpose, action and results.

Catch on Fire!
Telling others about God is at the very heart of the Christian life. Reignite the fire of your salvation and learn how to bring others into the Kingdom. A tremendous teaching on evangelism for our times.

Audiotapes

Prayer and Fasting
This four-tape series is an excellent companion to Kingsley Fletcher's book *Prayer and Fasting*, with new information not in the book.

Knowing Who You Are in Christ
We have an inheritance as sons and daughters of God, but we can tap into the victories He has for our lives only when we grasp His ultimate purpose for all believers. Eight tapes.

Covenant Relationships
This six-tape study explains how God has obligated Himself to fulfill His covenant promises and how He desires to bless His children. These revealing tapes are foundational to the book *The Power of Covenant*.

Keys to Your Success
When you learn the principles of success given in the Word, you can apply them to your daily life. "I pray that in all respects you may prosper and be in good health" (3 John 2). Six tapes.

The Anointing
An eight-tape study on the anointing and its power in our lives—what it is, why you need it, how to obtain it and how not to lose it. Learn how to be led by the Spirit on a daily basis. Powerful!

Experiencing God's Power
Be consumed with the zeal of the Lord and experience His power in your life! Learn how those who know the Lord will do great things in His name, and ignite everything in your path. Two tapes.

A Place Called There
There is a special place in God that not everyone has access to: the secret place of the Lord. Learn how to tap into it and advance in Him! Two tapes.

*For more information about these
and other resources by Kingsley Fletcher or to
place an order, write or call:*

KINGSLEY FLETCHER MINISTRIES

P.O. BOX 12017
RESEARCH TRIANGLE PARK, NC 27709-2017
PHONE: (919) 382-1944
INTERNET: WWW.KFMLIFE.ORG

Best-Sellers
from Regal

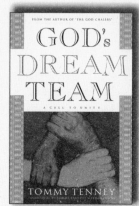
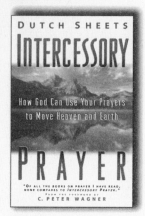

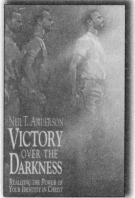
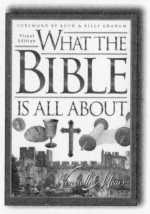